BED & BREAKFAST
AND
UNIQUE INNS
OF
Pennsylvania

BED & BREAKFAST
AND
UNIQUE INNS
OF
Pennsylvania

A Pictorial Guide
Photography by Bruce W. Muncy
Text by Linda C. Feltman

CRYSTAL SPRINGS
PUBLISHING

BED & BREAKFAST AND UNIQUE INNS OF
PENNSYLVANIA is published by Crystal Springs
Publishing, P.O. Box 8814, Roanoke, VA 24014.

First printed 1991

94 93 92 3 2 1

Printed in Hong Kong

Library of Congress Catalog Card Number 91-72066

ISBN 0-9620996-1-9 Soft Cover
ISBN 0-9620996-2-7 Hard Cover

Other books by Crystal Springs Publishing:
BED & BREAKFAST AND UNIQUE INNS OF
VIRGINIA

COVER PHOTOGRAPHS
top: Century Inn
bottom left to right:
Goose Chase Bed &
Breakfast,
Adamstown Inn

*The body travels more easily than the mind, and until we have
limbered up our imagination we continue to think as though we
had stayed at home. We have not really budged a step until we
take up residence in someone else's point of view.*

John Erskine

ACKNOWLEDGMENTS

Crystal Springs Publishing would like to acknowledge those individuals and agencies that gave so generously of their time, talents and skills.

Linda C. Feltman, researcher, author
Bruce W. Muncy, photographer, desk top publisher
Michael Barrus Muncy, managing editor, photography assistant
Lynn Davis, editorial editor
Dianne Smith, calligrapher, book designer
Elaine Lutz, assistant to the author

A special thanks to Governor Robert P. Casey for writing the Foreword and to the Department of Commerce, Bureau of Travel Marketing for writing the Introduction and for giving the publisher permission to use graphics and excerpts from state publications.

Also, a special thanks to Pennsylvania innkeepers for the gracious hospitality extended to us during our visits and for their flexibility in accommodating our sometimes inflexible schedules.

Quote by John Erskine reprinted with permission from the Middle Atlantic Press, Inc., 848 Church St., Wilmington, DE 19801.

Photograph on page 123 © Andrew A. Wagner
Portrait of Bruce W. Muncy © David Lesko

A NOTE FROM THE PUBLISHER

As a service to you, we have compiled in the back of the book a complete listing of Pennsylvania's inns. No one has paid to be in this list; it is for your use.

The pictured inns were selected by the author and publisher. Initial selection was based upon our firsthand knowledge and recommendations by travelers and other innkeepers. These inns were visited by the author and/or the publisher and photographed before the final selection was made. Some inns were eliminated.

The selected inns agreed to pay a portion of the production cost. We appreciate their financial assistance because without their help we could not produce a book of this size and quality and keep it affordable to you.

Many fine Pennsylvania B&B inns are not pictured due to space, but we have tried to present a sampling of the different styles, sizes and price offerings. We welcome your comments.

Please mail all inquiries and comments to Crystal Springs Publishing, P.O. Box 8814, Roanoke, VA 24014.

FOREWORD

Welcome to Pennsylvania. Where America declared her independence and framed our Constitution. Today, Pennsylvania offers you a virtually unlimited variety of historical sites, and an unrivaled selection of festivals, fairs and markets.

But there's more. Spectacular mountain vistas, great fishing and boating in streams and lakes and a wide array of outdoor activity. You'll find you're never very far from one of our 114 state parks. When the weather forces you indoors, you can enjoy the sights and sounds at hundreds of museums, theaters, dance companies and concerts.

Over 500 unique bed and breakfast and country inns in our state also offer you a little of everything. From a rural getaway on one of our picturesque farms to a quaint stay in one of our countless historic villages — each inn offers a unique experience. In this book you'll find all you'll need for a great vacation at one of our bed & breakfast or country inns. On behalf of Ellen and myself, and all Pennsylvanians, I extend our best wishes to you for a vacation filled with adventure and discovery. I'm sure that as you travel our beautiful and historic Commonwealth you'll agree that a great vacation starts here!

Robert P. Casey
Governor

CONTENTS

THE
EIGHT REGIONS
OF
Pennsylvania

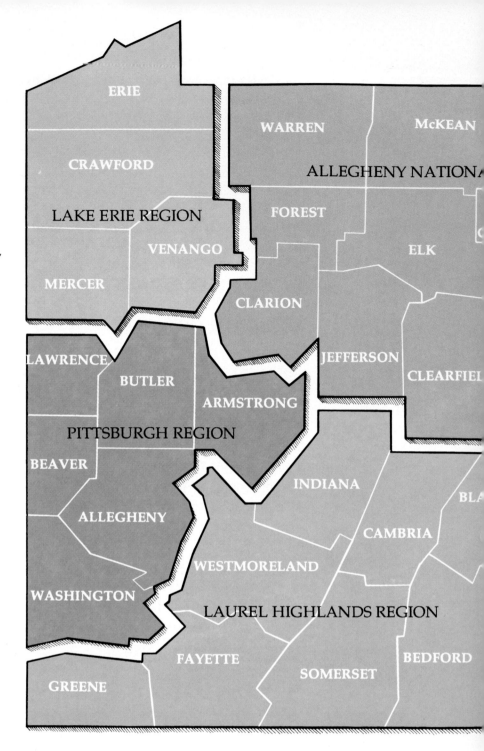

LAKE ERIE REGION

 There are more than 32,000 acres of inland lakes and hundreds of miles of rivers here, anchored by this region's greatest lake, Erie. History buffs won't want to miss Commodore Perry's U.S. Brig *Niagara*.

ALLEGHENY NATIONAL FOREST REGION

The centerpiece of this region is the Allegheny National Forest, a half million acres of paradise for nature lovers. This region also boasts The Magic Forests, plus more acres of state game land than anywhere else in the Commonwealth.

PITTSBURGH REGION

Visitors to this region will be amazed at the proximity of city to country. Just a short drive takes you from the tall spires of one of America's most spectacular urban skylines to Amish farmland and historic small towns.

LAUREL HIGHLANDS REGION

 The Allegheny Mountains small peaks of this region, making it a prime area for outdoor activities. The valleys below the highlands are filled with mining and manufacturing towns like Johnstown, part of America's Industrial Heritage Project.

HERSHEY / DUTCH COUNTRY REGION

 The golden fields of this region are home to Amish and Mennonite farmers who have cultivated this land for generations. There's also national history here: the famous Gettysburg battlefield and America's first capital, York. For present day fun there are the Reading shopping outlets and Hershey, "Chocolatetown. U.S.A."

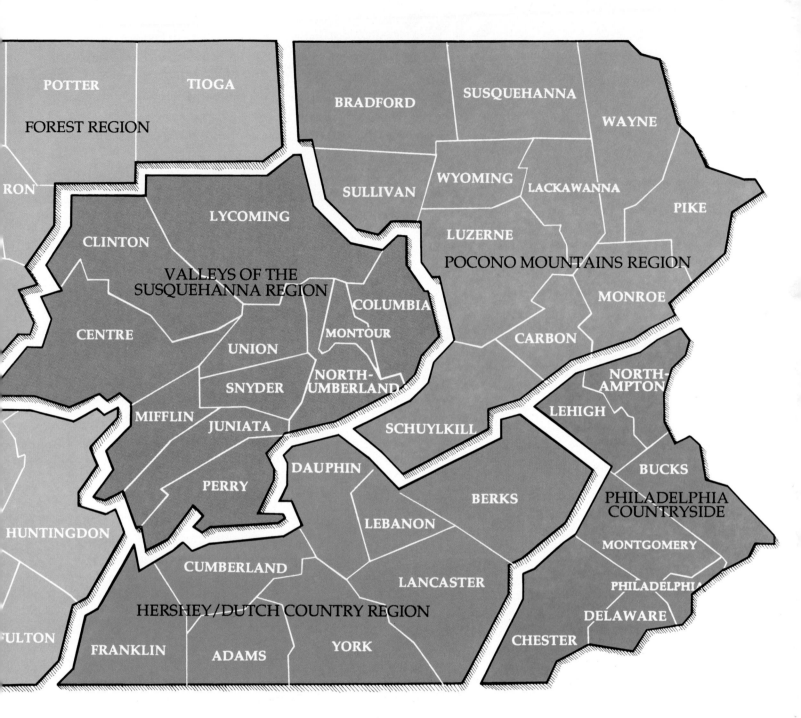

POTTER

TIOGA

FOREST REGION

BRADFORD

SUSQUEHANNA

WAYNE

RON

WYOMING

LACKAWANNA

PIKE

SULLIVAN

LYCOMING

LUZERNE

POCONO MOUNTAINS REGION

CLINTON

VALLEYS OF THE
SUSQUEHANNA REGION

COLUMBIA

MONROE

CENTRE

MONTOUR

UNION

CARBON

SNYDER

NORTH-
UMBERLAND

NORTH-
AMPTON

MIFFLIN

LEHIGH

JUNIATA

SCHUYLKILL

BUCKS

DAUPHIN

PERRY

BERKS

PHILADELPHIA
COUNTRYSIDE

HUNTINGDON

LEBANON

MONTGOMERY

CUMBERLAND

LANCASTER

PHILADELPHIA

HERSHEY/DUTCH COUNTRY REGION

DELAWARE

FULTON

FRANKLIN

ADAMS

YORK

CHESTER

POCONO MOUNTAINS REGION

Both the Endless and Pocono Mountains provide incredible scenic vista for nature lovers, and great challenges for skiers of every age. Hundreds of freshwater lakes mean spring and summer fun for boaters, swimmers and fishermen. And the towns of Scranton and Wilkes-Barre are alive with reminders of our industrial age.

VALLEYS OF THE SUSQUEHANNA REGION

Streams, creeks and rivers criss-cross this region. You'll find traditional river towns here, plus old mills and more covered bridges than anywhere else in the state. This region is also the home of the famous Nittany Lions of Penn State University.

PHILADELPHIA COUNTRYSIDE REGION

Here you'll find America's most historic square mile, including the Liberty Bell and Independence Hall, surrounded by one of our nation's most diverse cities. Outside the city are the lively artists' colonies of Bucks County, Bethlehem's Moravian settlements, Langhorne's Sesame Place amusement park and quaint towns along the Delaware River.

Pennsylvania

AMERICA STARTS HERE

When we say that America starts here in Pennsylvania, you'll recall immediately the events that created our country. It was here, at Independence Hall in Philadelphia, that America declared her independence and framed our Constitution. This is where the Liberty Bell first rang.

Among our 335 official historic sites is the Brandywine Battlefield, where Washington's army resisted the British occupation of Philadelphia. Washington Crossing Historic Park, where the Colonial Army crossed the Delaware on Christmas Day, 1776. And the city of York, America's first capital.

But all these famous places are only a small part of our story. The notion that America starts here doesn't begin and end with the founding of this nation; rather, it recognizes an ongoing record of achievement, a time line of accomplishment, that stretches from 1776 into the 1990s.

As the foundations of government were being laid, Pennsylvanians began establishing institutions that would become pillars of America's cultural life. Benjamin Franklin founded the country's first lending library. Philadelphians established the first American zoo, the first university, the first newspaper and the first savings bank.

The first American fire-fighting company, the Union, was started in 1736. Pennsylvania Hospital, founded in 1751, was this country's first independent hospital. The Philadelphia Stock Exchange was organized in 1790, two years before the New York Stock Exchange.

As some Pennsylvanians civilized the East, others struck out to settle the West. Colonel Henry Bouquet led the troops that defeated the Indians at Bushy Run Battlefield. Pittsburgh's Fort Pitt was the site of an important battle in the French and Indian War. Lake Erie was a proving ground for the young American Navy during the War of 1812. All these pivotal events went a long way toward opening the West.

That's why America's great move westward began right here in Pennsylvania. The Conestoga wagon was invented near Lancaster. The heavy traffic generated by these prairie schooners resulted in the nation's first rule of the road: "Drive on the right." This same traffic gave rise to an impressive network of roads, including America's first pike, Route 30, which today runs from Philadelphia to west of Pittsburgh.

While Pennsylvania's roads carried many people westward, many Old Order Amish and Mennonites were content to settle in central Pennsylvania. Establishing close-knit communities in Lancaster and Berks counties, they sought to live and farm without the distractions of modern life.

But soon a contemporary conflict intruded on this peaceful countryside. Located just north of the Mason-Dixon line, central Pennsylvania was the site of many Civil War battles. There were skirmishes near Carlisle. Chambersburg was the only Northern town burned by the Confederates during the war and Gettysburg was the site of the war's most terrible battle, where Yankee troops turned the tide and preserved the Union. If America started in Philadephia almost a century earlier, America was reborn on the Gettysburg battlefield.

At the same time, innovators and inventors across the Commonwealth were leading a second revolution, the Industrial Revolution. The first steam locomotive, the Stourbridge Lion, ran in Wayne County. The first steamship was built in Brownsville, Fayette County. Even the oil industry began here in 1859, near Oil Creek in Titusville.

With coal from the country's first anthracite mines and the railroads that carried it cross-country, towns like Scranton, Wilkes-Barre, Allentown and Altoona stoked the engines that drove America's industrial might. Cities like Pittsburgh and Johnstown helped us to produce more steel and iron than any other state at a time when our country's growth depended on vast quantities of both.

Another product of the industrial age was leisure time, and Pennsylvania led the way in finding new ways to have fun. As far back as 1815, travelers journeyed to the Pocono Mountains to enjoy the beautiful scenery, hike and ride along narrow mountain paths, and fish, swim and sail in hundreds of clear lakes.

For the 1876 World's Fair, a Pennsylvania pharmacist concocted a brew of herbs, bark and roots that sold as the first root beer. Pennsylvanians invented the Ferris wheel, the Slinky, the ice cream soda and the banana split.

At the turn of the 20th century, the first motion picture show in the world premiered in Philadelphia. Latrobe battled Jeannette in the first professional football game. The nation's first licensed radio station hit the airwaves in Pittsburgh. And Little League Baseball was founded in Williamsport.

As we stand on the brink of the 21st century, Pennsylvania continues to lead the nation in innovation. The computer was invented at the University of Pennsylvania. The electron microscope was invented in Allegheny County. The nation's first Robotics Institute was founded at Pittsburgh's Carnegie Mellon University in 1979.

The history of Pennsylvania's ingenuity runs from Benjamin Franklin's bifocals to the supercomputer, from this country's first cookbook to our Constitution. And so a trip through Pennsylvania will show you that history isn't just written by famous people in big cities. Instead, it's made by generations of hard-working people from every corner of the Commonwealth.

We invite you and your family to share both this rich past and exciting present. And we welcome you as you start your own special journey here, in Pennsylvania.

TIPS FOR THE DISCERNING TRAVELER

Bed and breakfast inns, once synonymous with European villages and cobblestone streets, have quickly become one of the fastest-growing segments of American tourism. Today, bed and breakfast inns are so alluring that even motels offering complimentary breakfasts call themselves "bed and breakfast motels."

With an increasing number of lodging establishments using the designation "bed and breakfast", it has become more and more difficult to determine with which type of B & B you are making reservations — a traditional inn which happens to include breakfast in the tariff, or a European-style B & B where you will be treated more like a house guest than a paying customer.

To mitigate the confusion somewhat, it may help to define several-general categories of B & B lodging (exceptions abound):

- homestays and Reservation Service Organizations (RSO's)
- B & B's
- country inns and urban inns

Homestays and **RSO's**, usually work hand-in-hand. By definition, a homestay is similar to the European version of B & B's. From the outside, the home is indistinguishable from other houses in the area. Homestay hosts advertise by listing with an RSO, an American innovation that has only recently caught on in Europe. The RSO typically represents 50 to 200 carefully screened and inspected properties and will arrange lodging according to your specific needs.

B & B's are generally identifiable by at least one sign on the property and advertise in the local and national media. More often than not the innkeeper is the owner and resides at the B & B. Sometimes the term "inn" is added after B & B. These B & B inns may offer evening meals for guests.

The **country inn** or **urban inn** often has a full-service restaurant, with as many as 25 guest rooms, usually with private baths. Guests are greeted at a front desk by an official innkeeper who is usually not the owner.

Whatever type of B & B you select, you need to book early especially for the peak times. Before calling the B & B, make a list of what you like and don't like. You may want to check on pet restrictions, the existence of in-residence pets, stairs, bed size, dietary considerations, restrictions on children, special parking (an RV needs extra space), a private bath, check-in and check-out times, and smoking and alcohol policies. If you inform your host of your needs, you help insure an enjoyable and memorable visit.

When you make your reservation, expect to guarantee the room with a deposit. Policies will vary, some B & B's require guests to forward a personal check within a specified time period; others accept a credit card deposit. The amount required will differ among B & B's, but in most cases a minimum of one night's stay is the requested deposit.

Should you cancel the reservation and miss the predetermined cancellation deadline, such as "less than five days before the date that you were to arrive," be prepared to forfeit at least $5 to $15, and the entire deposit.

Once you check in, your stay will be enhanced if you remember to be considerate of others. The most sensitive subject is probably the bathroom. If you are sharing a bath in the hall with other guests don't forget your bathrobe. Remember that other guests may be waiting and leave the bathroom as you found it.

Consideration is the key in other matters as well. For instance, long distance calls should be made collect or with a calling-card number. There are no obligations or rules for gratuities, but innkeepers who employ housekeepers may sometimes leave a tray or envelop for guests who wish to leave a tip.

Knowing what to expect insures a pleasurable stay. Innkeepers enjoy people. That's why they are in the business. When you discover the special hospitality, charm and personal attention innkeepers lavish on their guests, you'll realize why the B & B movement has been so successful.

R epresenting host properties located throughout the southeastern corridor of Pennsylvania, Lucy and Peggy offer the traveling public more than 50 pre-inspected bed and breakfast homestays and small inns.

The private homeowners, who have chosen not to advertise their hospitality through conventional media, list with Bed & Breakfast Connections because of the owners' expertise in matching guest needs with hosts.

From the diverse selection of properties, guests may choose a country farmhouse, a downtown high-rise or an historic mansion. Since each property is personally inspected, guests will always find an inviting atmosphere and hosts who give personal attention to their comfort and needs.

BED & BREAKFAST CONNECTIONS RSO

Peggy Gregg & Lucy Scribner

Box 21, Devon, PA 19333. Phone: (215) 687-3565 or (800) 448-3619 (outside PA), best to call 9 a.m. - 9 p.m., Monday - Saturday, or 1 - 9 p.m., Sunday, answering machine other times. Locations include the greater Philadelphia area, including Historic Center City, Revolutionary Valley Forge, the scenic Brandywine Valley and rolling hills of Pennsylvania Dutch Country.

PHILADELPHIA COUNTRYSIDE

Details

Check in and out: noon. Deposit/Cancellation Policy: one night plus handling fee plus tax deposit. Deposit refunded, less a $15 service charge if cancellation is received seven days or more prior to arrival date. No refund if cancellation is received with less than seven days' notice. Forfeiture of deposit is avoided by rescheduling and staying with the same host within a three-month period. Payment: personal check, MasterCard, VISA, or American Express. Policies regarding children, smoking, pets and other considerations vary from property to property.

Rates

$40 - $160 double occupancy. Suites to $190. Extra person, when permitted, $10 - $20.

Weekly and monthly rates. Two-night minimum stay for certain hosts and occasional special events. $5 surcharge for a one-night stay. Reservation fee of $2 for one-night stay, $5 for stays of more than one night.

Bed & Bath

The variety and scope of guest rooms available fulfill any traveler's needs. Call or write for detailed listing of entire host roster.

Extra Facilities & Features

Many hosts can accommodate small business meetings, wedding receptions, or corporate retreats. Fax and in-room phones at some locations.

INN AT LIGHTEDHOLLY

ocated in the main street community of Kennett Square, this 1850s Federal-style brick home is within walking distance of many quaint shops and fine restaurants. During the Civil War, Kennett Square was an important link in the underground railroad and today claims the title of Mushroom Capital of the U.S.

For the Zinners, finding this colonial townhouse satisfied the dream of operating a bed and breakfast. When it came time to choose a name for their inn, Carolyn's love of her red holly china, a gift from her mother, plus the presence of a holly bush, now draped year-round in twinkling white lights, set the theme for the bed and breakfast.

One aspect they like to emphasize is the extra safety and homelike comforts available to travelers choosing a bed and breakfast for their lodging. An experienced business traveler herself, Carolyn says she seeks out bed and breakfasts whenever possible for this reason.

Carolyn & Peter Zinner

216 N. Union St. Kennett Square, PA 19348. Phone: (215) 444-9246, best to call before 11 a.m. or after 6 p.m., answering machine other times. Location: Chester County, on Route 82, 11 miles from Wilmington, DE, and 4 miles from Route 1. Five-minute drive to Longwood Gardens.

Details

Check in: after 6 p.m. Check out: 11 a.m. Deposit/Cancellation Policy: credit card guarantee or one night's deposit. Deposit refunded less $20 if cancellation made four days prior to reservation and room is rebooked. Payment: cash, personal checks, MasterCard, and VISA. Infants or children over 7 welcome. No smoking or guest pets. In residence: a llasa-poo, Muffy. Central air conditioning. Limited off-street parking, ample on-street parking in front of house.

Rates

$70 - $90 double occupancy. Two-night minimum stay on holiday weekends. Best to call one month in advance.

Bed & Bath

Three guest rooms. One with private bath, working fireplace, and a queen-size, four-poster bed. Two other rooms have queen-size beds, traditional furnishings and share a hallway bath. Antique bedspreads in summer, goose-down comforters in winter. Feather pillows, phone jacks (phones upon request) in rooms.

Breakfast & Extras

Served in a candlelit dining room on an elegantly appointed table including the holly-patterned china, a breakfast featuring freshly baked fruit-filled turnovers, home-baked bread, fresh fruit, juice, coffee, or tea. Evenings, guests will find a snack basket in the hallway filled with cookies, chocolate and fruit.

Built in 1715, this whitewashed stone farmhouse has watched British troops take off with the owner's food stuffs to feed the troops awaiting the battle of Brandywine. Later it was part of the underground railroad. Used as a summer home in the late 1800s, it serves now as a peaceful retreat in all seasons for folks seeking a quiet refuge from busy city life.

As guests turn into the long country lane marked by a post and rail fence, they will be greeted by manicured grounds and majestic 150-year old trees guarding an expansive ten acres of rolling countryside. Along with the adjacent 400-acre Nature Conservancy, there are well-marked bird, hiking and cross-country ski trails.

On cold days guests frequently gather in front of the kitchen's wood-stove over a cup of hot chocolate and some good conversation.

WHITETHORNE

James & Marianne Hoy

1778 Unionville and Wawaset Road (Route 842), Box 92, Unionville, PA 19375. Phone: (215) 793-1748, anytime, answering machine if not available. Location: Chester County, 5 miles west of West Chester and 3 miles east of Unionville on Route 842, five minutes from Longwood Gardens.

PHILADELPHIA COUNTRYSIDE

Details

Check in: 4 - 6 p.m. Check out: 12 noon. Deposit/Cancellation. Policy: one night's deposit. Refunded, less a 20% processing fee with seven days' notice for cancellations. Payment: cash, personal check, or VISA. Children 3 and over. No smoking. Guest pets may use barn or nearby kennels. No handicap access. Window air conditioners.

Rates

$70 - $75 double occupancy. $10 for additional person. Sleeping bag, extra charge applies. Two night minimum weekends.

Bed & Bath

Three rooms. Maid's Quarters has antique pineapple double bed, private bath. Lisa's Room has an antique canopy double bed, and shares bath with King Room which has a reproduction colonial four-poster bed.

Breakfast & Extras

Served in formal dining room, kitchen with woodburning stove, or on patio in full view of grounds, an unusual breakfast that alternately features eggs, fresh flounder with cheddar cheese sauce, chilled asparagus with tomatoes, and hearts of palm with a vinaigrette dressing or a cream cheese and strawberry-stuffed French toast, made with an eggnog and Grand Marnier batter topped with hot strawberry sauce. Juice and beverages.

Extra Facilities & Features

Use of a canoe and two ten-speed bikes, hot air balloon rides (pre-arranged - additional charge) and carriage rides. Stables for guest's horses. During hunting season, guests can "follow the hunt." Grounds ideal for weddings.

COACHAUS

ong before major hotel chains began moving towards the suite concept, Barbara bought and restored five of Allentown's brick buildings, all previously owned by 19th century businessmen. Now, from the outside, what appears to be a single row home is actually a European-style small inn that has the feel of a gracious home with the amenities of a fine hotel. By linking the five buildings, Barbara created a unique property with tastefully appointed guest rooms, suites with sitting rooms and kitchens, and a selection of two-bedroom apartments and three-bedroom townhouses perfect for families with small children.

This uniquely flexible choice of accommodations has made the Coachaus an oasis for business travelers. The main dining room becomes a productive meeting place. Here, over breakfast or during the evening gathering, guests have a chance to meet with other travelers. And because the Coachaus regularly welcomes guests from the four corners of the world, it provides an unusual opportunity to chat with international visitors in a casual setting.

The convenient location allows guests to walk to area restaurants, shops and historical sites. Nearby are the Old Allentown Historic District, the Liberty Bell Shrine, the Allentown Art Museum and other architectural sites of note.

Details

Check in: 1 p.m. Check out: 12 noon. Deposit/Cancellation Policy: no deposit required if guaranteed by credit card. 24 hours' notice cancellations. Payment: cash, personal check, MasterCard, VISA, American Express, Diners, or Carte Blanche. Accommodations for children and guest pets available on a limited basis and with advance notice. Smoking permitted in designated areas, but no pipes or cigars. In residence: dalmatian, Abby. No handicap access. Central air conditioning. Off-street parking available and non-metered parking after 5 p.m.

Rates

$74 - $78 double occupancy. $90 - $125 for suites. Extra person in room $10. Extra beds $20. Crib per night $10. Two to four weeks' notice advised for holidays and weekends.

Bed &Bath

Ten guest rooms and 14 suites, all with color-coordinated private baths. Bedrooms have either queen- or king-size beds. Suites have fully equipped kitchens and sitting rooms. All have television, telephones and alarm clocks. Two have balconies, six have private terraces. Each guest area has been restored in a classic style using appropriate furnishings and warm color-coordinated accessories.

Breakfast & Extras

Served in nicely appointed dining room, a full breakfast of ham, sausage, bacon, selection of cereals, assorted breads, eggs cooked to individual order, and juice, coffee, or tea. Evenings feature an "attitude adjustment hour" from 6 to 7 p.m., helping guests to relax after a busy day.

Extra Facilities & Features

Conference space available for up to eight participants. Fax available. Catering for lunches and dinners can be arranged. Special corporate rate. With the Coachaus' emphasis on privacy, it is well-suited for smaller scale business meetings and personal interviews. Also perfect for executives relocating to Lehigh Valley while waiting to move into their new home. Whether it be advice on schools, physicians, or any one of the things a resident might take for granted, Barbara and her staff can help.

Barbara Kocher

107 - 111 North Eighth St., Allentown, PA 18101. Phone: (215) 821-4854 or (800) 762-8680. Location: Lehigh County, in the heart of Allentown. Use Seventh Street exit off Route 22. Go 1 1/4 miles to Linden Street and turn right. Go 1 block and turn right on N. Eighth Street.

EVERMAY ON THE DELAWARE

In a letter to the Society of Free Trade in 1683, William Penn speaks of a Buckingham County, a name chosen perhaps as a dedication to family and friends remaining behind in Penn's motherland, Buckinghamshire, England. One of three original counties established by Penn in 1682, Bucks County, as it is known today, represents a microcosm of Pennsylvania's history.

Dating back to the 1700s, Evermay on the Delaware has been witness to much history. Located on 25 acres of pastures, woodland, and gardens between the Delaware River and Canal, it was extensively remodeled in 1871 to serve as an inn, and has welcomed visitors ever since.

The current owners purchased it in 1981. Their continual dedication to detail and total lack of self-promotion have fostered an environment that often surprises first-time guests with its understated elegance.

Relaxation begins the moment a guest steps into the entrance hall. The day's missed deadlines and snarled traffic become distant memories as Ron and Fred offer a glass of sherry or cup of tea, accompanied by the soothing background strains of Mozart.

Dinner, prepared by Ron — who has cooked at LaVerenne in Paris and with the late James Beard in New York — prompts regular comments from guests that it was a highlight of their stay.

A summer morning stroll reveals gardens brimming with flowers and pastures teeming with iridescent peacocks and black-faced sheep.

Details

Check in: 2 p.m. Check out: 12 noon. Deposit/Cancellation Policy: equivalent to one night's stay sent, applied to last day of intended stay, refunded with seven days' notice. Payment: cash, personal check, MasterCard, or VISA. Children over 12 welcome. Smoking permitted in designated areas, no cigars or pipes. Unsuitable for guest pets. Handicap access. Air conditioning units in all guest rooms. Central air conditioning on first floor and dining areas. Off-street parking.

Rates

$75 - $135. $175 for two-bedroom suites. $20 additional person in room. Dinner is $45 per person. Best to call two months in advance for peak weekends and holidays. Two-night booking required if stay includes Saturday. Three nights required on holidays.

Bed & Bath

Sixteen guest rooms in the manor house, carriage house, and cottage, 14 with private bath in room, two with private bath in hall, each named after a character of historical or cultural significance to the owners. Rooms are decorated with Victorian antiques and collectibles, most with double beds. Exceptions include the Pearl S. Buck Room with king-size bed and Chief Nutimus Loft with a queen-size bed. The Redfield is a two-bedroom suite with one double bed in each room and a private bath featuring a clawfoot tub. Some rooms have a separate sitting room. Other features are cathedral windows, oriental rugs and fireplaces. Fresh fruit and flowers are in rooms, turn-down service, cordials and chocolates in rooms upon retiring.

Breakfast & Extras

Served in the conservatory, a compote of fresh fruit, variety of croissants, muffins, juice and coffee. Complimentary copies of *New York Times* at breakfast. Box lunches can be ordered for the day's country outing. Afternoon tea is served at 4 p.m. in the parlor and, during warmer months, on the patio. Dinner is one seating at 7:30, served Friday, Saturday, Sunday, and holidays. It is prix fixe; menu changes daily, begins with aperitifs and hors d'oeuvres, followed by six courses with a choice of entrees. Entrees may include poached salmon with lobster sauce, grilled yellowfin tuna or roast loin of veal with lentils. Guests staying the weekend are asked to reserve one evening meal during their visit.

Extra Facilities & Features

Space available for weekday corporate conferences and retreats for up to 20 participants. Fax and PC plug-ins available. Catering for lunch and dinner can be arranged. Special corporate rate. Appropriate for small weddings Sunday through Friday. Delaware tow path abuts property; ideal for an extended stroll or cross-country skiing.

Ronald Strouse & Frederick Cresson

River Road, Erwinna, PA 18920. Phone: (215) 294-9100, best to call 8:30 a.m. - 10:00 p.m., but phone is personally answered 24 hours. Location: Bucks County, 13 1/2 miles north of New Hope on Route 32.

GLASBERN

Situated in the open meadows of a 100-year-old farm, this post-and-beam Pennsylvania German bank-barn has been reconstructed from an 1800s foundation, shale wall, and hand-hewn wooden beams, to become the Barn, the main house of Glasbern. Visitors will notice the high, vaulted ceiling of the Great Room and the pleasing geometical relationships of the Barn's ladders to the hay mow.

The Carriage House and Farmhouse offer separate accommodations from those available in the Barn.

Within a few miles of Allentown's growing business and cultural scene, Glasbern provides a serene, pastoral setting, ideal for a peaceful retreat from the rapid pace of modern living.

The 100 acres of farmland with trails along three streams and two ponds provide a wide array of activities for weekend vacationers. Visitors will also discover the area offers cycling events and tours, paths and wildlife sanctuaries, historic festivals, and covered bridge tours.

The Grangers, who left careers in business and education to live the country life, say they are working harder than ever while enjoying it at least twice as much.

Details

Check in: 4 p.m. Check out: 12 noon. Deposit/Cancellation Policy: first night of stay credited to last day of intended stay. Seven days' cancellation notice for weekend stays. Payment: cash or personal check preferred, but MasterCard, VISA, American Express accepted. Limited accommodations for children. Unsuitable for guest pets. Cigarette smoking is permitted, but no cigars or pipes. On premises: friendly retriever, Chessy. Six rooms are handicap accessible. Central air conditioning. Off-street parking.

Rates

$100 - $200 for guest rooms. $150 - $200 for suites. $15 extra person in room. Two-night minimum for suites with whirlpool and fireplace on weekends and holidays. Best to call at least two weeks in advance for reservations.

Bed & Bath

Ten guest rooms and 11 suites, all with queen- or king-size beds, private baths, telephones, and televisions. 14 have whirlpool baths and seven have working fireplaces. Rooms with whirlpools have terry robes provided. Besides guest rooms in the Barn, separate guest areas and suites include Glasbern's Carriage House — continuing the theme of country textures set in contemporary comfort, with skylighted sunrooms, king and queen-size beds, fireplaces, and whirlpools in each of the four rooms. Nestled close to a meandering stream, the Farmhouse features three suites with whirlpools, fireplaces, and sitting areas. Guest suites on the ground floor of the Barn feature whirlpools in inviting sunrooms, and each has a private entrance which leads to the terraced yard and swimming pool overlooking the meadows.

Breakfast & Extras

Served in the cathedral setting of the Great Room, guests visit by the fireplace while enjoying a full country breakfast of whole-wheat pancakes or bacon and eggs with fruit, cereal, coffee cake, juice and hot beverages. Evening dining is available Tuesday through Saturday with overnight guests receiving priority for reservations. Chef Mark Shields studied at Le Cordon Bleu de Paris; the menu features country French cuisine.

Extra Facilities & Features

Excellent site for corporate conferences. Space available for 20 participants. Fax and PC plug-ins available. Meals prepared by the chef at Glasbern.

Beth & Al Granger

Packhouse Road, Box 250, Fogelsville, PA 18051. Phone: (215) 285-4723 or (800) 654-9296, before 11 p.m., answering machine when not available. Location: Lehigh County, 10 miles west of Allentown via Route 22/78, off Route 9, North East Extension, Lehigh Valley Interchange.

GUESTHOUSES
R S O

icture a beautiful, secluded 40-acre country estate built on the hills rising above the Delaware River. Mix one frazzled urban couple with one weekend at Pleasant Hill. Impossible deadlines, congested traffic and foul-smelling smog become distant memories.

At Pleasant Hill, the hosts' entire raison d'etre is to create a luxuriously restful weekend for city dwellers caught in the rat race of the crazy corporate world. Particularly adept at relating to their guests' needs, the hosts offer flexibility in schedules and meals when needed and provide a pampered, soothing atmosphere that encourages guests to unwind.

Besides the hosts' gracious hospitality, their home offers guests a haven of unusual beauty with its spacious and unique design. One of the most dramatic rooms is the Great Room where guests are often found curled up next to the two-story stone fireplace, reading a good book or listening to music. Several hundred additional acres surround the property, thus ensuring a quiet restful retreat.

The secluded location belies the fact that Pleasant Hill is only minutes away from quaint villages and tourist attractions. Visitors to these river villages should bring their walking shoes, since the Delaware's tow paths provide miles of scenic walkway year-round.

Details

Check in: flexible. Check out: 12 noon. Deposit/Cancellation Policy: credit card guarantee of first and last nights' lodging. If canceled more than five days prior to visit, full credit of deposit is applied to future visit within one year. To be eligible for money to be returned, trip cancellation insurance must be applied for at the time of reservation. Information also sent with confirmation. Payment: cash, personal check, MasterCard, VISA, or American Express. Children welcome in separate Carriage House. No smoking. Unsuitable for guest pets. Central air conditioning.

Rates

$125 - $175 double occupancy for three suites. $175 for Carriage House. Sleeping bags permitted in Carriage House. Additional $20 charge applies for each additional person in Carriage House.

Bed & Bath

Three bright, sunny guest suites and separate Carriage House. All have private baths, queen-size beds, each specially constructed and decorated in a theme. All offer unusual privacy. Special features include the whirlpool and jacuzzi in the Silver Suite and the Roma Suite's in-ground Roman tub. The stone Carriage House, original to the property, has a full kitchen, dining area, and a living room with fireplace that is two stories tall. Ample wood pile just outside. The upstairs guest room has a peaked ceiling and queen-size bed. Furnishings vary from antique to contemporary and always freshly appointed with flowering greenery from the estate's greenhouse.

Breakfast & Extras

Served in the formal dining room, a hearty country breakfast with menu choices dependent upon guests' whims and desires. A typical main course may include anything from apple pancakes to filled fritatas. Accompaniments include assorted muffins and cereals, fresh fruit compote, juice and beverages. When families use the Carriage House, the kitchen is stocked with breakfast foods. In the main house, the Great Room has a buffet available day or night featuring fresh fruit, crackers, cheese, nuts and candies to satisfy those unexpected munchie attacks!

Pleasant Hill

For reservations, contact: Guesthouses, Inc., Box 2137, West Chester, PA 19380. Phone: (215) 692-4575 or (800) 950-9130; 12 noon - 4 p.m. Monday - Friday. Fax: (215) 692-4451. For more information on Guesthouses, Inc., and other properties available through this reservation service, please see separate description. Location of Pleasant Hill: Bucks County, northwest of Route 32 (River Road) and Lambertville Bridge (Delaware River) by 5 miles.

GUESTHOUSES
R S O

$\mathfrak{G}$uesthouses, Inc. is a Bed & Breakfast Reservation Service and Broker for special events and services. The company was formed to represent private owners of historic, National Register or Landmark properties. These properties have usually been in the family for decades, if not for generations.

Guesthouses also represents bed and breakfast inns, small hotels and independent hosts. All properties meet the *Gold Medallion* international standard of gracious hospitality established by the non-profit trade association, Bed & Breakfast World-Wide.

One of the first members of Guesthouses, Hamanassett, (the Native American word for "meeting place"), is just north of Chadd's Ford. As guest ascend Hamanassett's half-mile driveway, they are treated to a stunning display of ancient flowering shrubs and perennials overseen by the host, a Philadelphia Flower Show prize-winner. The host's family has lived on this 38-acre Pennsylvania Historic Property since the early 1800s. The stone mansion still has its original furnishings.

Another Guesthouses property, Lenni, also near Chadd's Ford, is named for the Brandywine tribe of American Indian. The estate, a Landmark site, was constructed of green serpentine stone in the Italianate style during the mid-1800s. The interior furnishings and decorations are faithful to this period.

Details

Check in: flexible. Check out: 12 noon. Deposit/Cancellation Policy: World-Wide member accommodations guaranteed; if guest arrives but does not take occupancy, for any reason, no charge and any monies paid refunded in full. Deposits by check or money order (received by Guesthouses within five days of request) or guarantees by MasterCard, Visa, or American Express for first and last nights' lodging required. Cancellations must be received by five days prior to scheduled arrival for guests to receive full credit for deposit. Credit applied to future visit to same host within one year. To be eligible for returned money, trip cancellation insurance must be obtained at time of reservation or on receipt of confirmation (12 days or more prior to arrival date). Guesthouses will help you select a suitable accommodation from its varied list.

Rates

$40-$200+ Double occupancy: $10 discounted for single occupancy. Increased by $20-$50 per extra person, where available. One-night discount on a weekly stay given at most host properties. Greater discounts given on stays of 31 nights or more at selected accommodations.

Bed and Bath

Hamanassett has four comfortably furnished, over-sized rooms with private baths on the second and third floors. Two suites: one with two bedrooms, living room and bath; the other with one bedroom, two full-size beds, sitting room and bath. All rooms provided with television, trays of refreshments and fresh flowers.
Lenni has large, corner guest rooms on the second floor; all have fireplaces. The third floor suite has living room with fireplace/woodstove, private bath and kitchenette, which can be stocked for a private breakfast.

Breakfast & Extras

At Hamanssett expect memorable breakfasts in the Georgian dining room. The host is a graduate of the Cordon Bleu.
Lenni provides a full country breakfast in the formal dining room or, if guests prefer to mingle with the cooks, by an antique pot-bellied stove in the kitchen. Afternoon tea may be served in the Grand Salon, the Library, the tower Hunt Room or outside on the Loggia, which overlooks the ten acres of lawn.

Extra Facilities & Features

Package holidays for two: "Brandywine Breakaways" and "Valley Forge Vacation" include historic lodgings; prix-fixe dinner at a historic inn; tickets to the area's museums, gardens and historic sites; plus surprises. Guest Yachts: B & B on the Chesapeake Bay aboard one of more than 30 sailing vessels. Location broker: for film and television productions and advertising in the print and television media. Special events broker: for location and hospitality for weddings, parties, foundation and corporate meetings, retreats, and incentive vacations. Theme package for groups: "Manor House Murders" and "Polo and Pimms" are two of the more than ten themes offered here; described by Arthur Frommer as "...the most unique vacation in the U.S."

Guesthouses, Inc.
Janice Archbold

Box 2137, West Chester, PA 19380. Phone (215) 692-4575 or (800) 950-9130 noon - 4 p.m., Monday-Friday. Fax (215) 692-4451. Location: Pennsylvania, Delaware, New Jersey, Maryland, and Washington D.C. and selected countries (for which no fee is charged).

ISAAC STOVER HOUSE

At one point in Alice's Adventures in Wonderland, Alice longs to go live in The Looking-Glass House — she was absolutely certain it would be "quite different . . . with oh such beautiful things in it." Walking through the bright red door at the Isaac Stover House is a little bit like what Alice had envisioned: it is different and it is beautiful.

Perhaps because talk show host and inveterate collector Sally Jesse Raphael had run out of new challenges, or because she had simply run out of space for her seemingly limitless collections, she purchased this 1837 Federal Victorian. There she proceeded to preside over its storybook transformation. In just three short months, the austere interior became a theatrical stage-like setting, brimming with countless globe-trotting treasures and an incomparable display of Victoriana.

The capricious mixture of flea-market discoveries, auction finds, unusual collectibles, and worldly treasures creates a delightful sort of organized chaos. It is true to the Victorian period and as pleasing to the eye as it is fun to touch and examine.

However, it would take considerably longer than the average weekend visit to appreciate the full extent of the wonderful things filling every nook and cranny. A world map wouldn't hurt either.

A dauntless traveler, Sally has collected bounty from every country that permits American citizens to cross its borders, and even a few that don't!

The Isaac Stover House overlooks the Delaware from 13 acres of meadows and woods. Named for a prominent Erwinna family, it welcomes travelers visiting the woods and farmlands, flea markets and antique shops of historic Bucks County.

Details

Check in: 4 p.m. Check out: 12 noon. Deposit/Cancellation Policy: a deposit of one night's lodging sent, refunded, less a $10 handling charge, with seven days' notice of shortening or cancelling reservation. Payment: cash or personal check preferred. MasterCard, VISA, or American Express accepted. Children over 12 welcome. Unsuitable for guest pets. Smoking permitted in common areas. No handicap access. Air conditioned. Ceiling fans in bedrooms. In residence: angora calico, Precious; green opinionated parrot, Lord Rumbottom, quartered in the greenhouse, and Bunny FooFoo resides outside.

Rates

$150 - $175 double occupancy. $250 bridal suite. Additional person $15. Two-night minimum stay on weekends and three-night minimum stay holidays. Limited number of Friday-only reservations available.

Bed & Bath

Five guest rooms plus two-room suite, all with Victorian-era double beds and furnishings, five with private bath and two share a bath. The whimsical names fulfill nostalgic and fairytale-like themes. Only the yellow brick road is missing from the Emerald City Room, with its Judy Garland photos, prevalence of Oz characters, and the sign with Dorothy's "Gee, Toto, I don't think we're in Kansas anymore." Another second floor room is the red, blue and white Loyalty Royalty Room, filled with memorabilia from Britain and the colonies, including a Daughters of American Revolution certificate. A snapshot from Jackie Gleason's "The Honeymooners" and more than two dozen Norman Rockwell plates set the theme for the two-room Bridal Suite. Both the Loyalty Royalty Room and the Bridal Suite have fireplaces and river views. Third floor rooms include the Amore Room, the Secret Garden Room, based on F. H. Burnett's children's classic, and the Cupids Bower Room where the preponderance of frilly lace, green, pink and gold gilt accents create the feeling of having just stepped inside a Valentine. Treasures from every corner of the globe accent each room.

Breakfast & Extras

Served fireside in the formal dining area on cloth-covered ice cream parlor tables, a typical breakfast of freshly baked lemon bread, fruit compote, granola, cranberry-apricot juice, and an Isaac Stover egg specialty such as French stuffed toast or a potato cheese fritata. The greenhouse is a favorite gathering place to enjoy an afternoon cup of tea. When late night hunger strikes, guests are encouraged to raid the cookie jar, filled each day with Sue's special cookies. The chocolate chip cookies disappear almost as fast as she can bake them. Swiss chocolates left bedside for sweet dreams.

Extra Facilities & Features

Conference space available for up to 20 participants. Corporate rate. Picnics planned upon request. Theater service available.

Sue Tettemer, *Innkeeper*
Sally Jesse Raphael, *Owner*

P. O. Box 68, Route 32, Erwinna, PA 18920. Phone: (215) 294-8044, call anytime, answering machine on occasion. Location: Bucks County, on Route 32, 13 miles north of New Hope.

JOSEPH AMBLER INN

Using part of a 150-acre site obtained from William Penn, Joseph Ambler, a skilled wheelwright, built a small 1 1/2-story home of fieldstone and wood in 1734. Nearly 100 years later in 1820, John Robert, who married an Ambler descendant, added the 2 1/2-story center section and porch. For posterity, he cut his name into one of the front stones. He also erected a large stone barn next to his home. In 1929, the Wright family added a third section. They also constructed a small house for their tenant farmer, which is now the Corybeck guest cottage.

As guests approach the long, winding drive, they are struck by the peaceful, pastoral setting of the fine country estate, a world of its own, with 12 rolling acres of meadows, manicured lawns and well-tended gardens.

Inside, the elegance and fine finishing touches of the past are everywhere. Guests are encouraged to enjoy three living rooms in the main house and to wander through the large school room with its massive walk-in fireplace, part of the original 1734 section. Here a fire blazes each night in winter.

One superlative of the inn is its truly excellent food served at the barn restaurant, which is divided into three separate areas. The professional chef serves some delectable dishes that every palate will savor.

Whether it's for a romantic weekend away or an important business conference, the Joseph Ambler Inn has all the delightful features one would expect of a great inn rooted in the past.

Details

Check in: 3 p.m. Check out: 11 a.m. Deposit/Cancellation Policy: one night paid in advance, full refund if cancelled ten days prior to reservation. Payment: cash, personal check, MasterCard, VISA, American Express, Diners Club, or Discover. Smoking is unrestricted, except pipes and cigars only in bar area. Children welcome. Unsuitable for guest pets. Kennels nearby. In residence: preschooler, Caitlin. Two guest rooms and restaurant are handicap accessible. Central air conditioning. Off-street parking.

Rates

$92 - $140 double occupancy. $20 for extra person in room. Children's sleeping bags permitted, extra charge applies. Best to call one-two months in advance for holiday weekends.

Bed & Bath

Twenty-four guest rooms and four suites, all with private baths in room, telephone, television, and double or queen-size beds. All are variably furnished with a tasteful selection of fine antiques, oriental rugs, carefully selected window treatments and many fine finishing touches. Located in three areas on property: the 1734 stone manor main house has six rooms on second and third floors plus three suites including a first floor bridal suite with private entrance. The Corybeck was once the tenant farmer's cottage. The name refers to the yearly migration of crows and black birds to property. There are now seven rooms, five with ground-floor private entrance and two located on the second floor. The 1820 stone bank-barn houses five rooms and one suite on the second floor and six rooms on the third floor. Each room opens into a large center hallway framed at one end by a magnificent two-story window. Many of the guest rooms have exposed stone walls and each has its own heat and air conditioning controls.

Breakfast & Extras

Served in one of several carefully appointed colonial dining areas located in the renovated stone barn, a delicious breakfast of Joseph Ambler Inn: French toast, country sausage, French omelettes, fruit, Danish and beverages. Elegant evening dining is also available with a menu featuring artfully prepared nouveau and traditional American cuisine.

Extra Facilities & Features

Excellent meeting and banquet facilities for up to 50 participants in cathedral ceiling conference room. Huge windows and French doors look out on the manicured lawns and gardens. The adjoining bar is handcrafted from original barn timbers. Special lunch and dinners can be arranged. Special corporate rate for guest rooms and use of conference facilities.

Terry & Steve Kratz,
Innkeepers
Richard P. Allman, Owner

1005 Horsham Road (Route 463), North Wales, PA 19454. Phone: (215) 362-7500, 24 hours a day. Location: Montgomery County, 7 miles from PA Turnpike Exit 26, 1 mile east of Montgomeryville intersection of Route 202, 309 and 463.

THOMAS BOND HOUSE

fter a climb up the steep winding staircase and a walk down the narrow lantern-lit hallways to the quaint 18th century guest rooms, it's not hard to imagine the history these walls could tell.

Built in 1769 for Dr. Thomas Bond, personal physcian of Benjamin Franklin, this four-story red brick home is now part of the Independence National Historical Park.

Bond and Franklin no doubt had many late-night discussions in the parlor about the volatile political atmosphere in the Colonies. Perhaps when their friend Benjamin Rush joined them, discussions turned to the success of the Pennsylvania Hospital, the nation's first public hospital, chartered in 1751 and founded by these three men.

The home had additions built in 1824 and 1840 and is now a restored landmark. A historical architect was hired to maintain the authenticity of the 18th-century restoration.

Thomas Bond, is within easy walking distance of 18th-century Philadelphia, Pennsylvania's largest city and the birthplace of all the ideals Washington's army fought to preserve. Here visitors can walk to the Liberty Bell Pavilion, Independence Hall and Betsy Ross's home.

On the ground level of the Thomas Bond House is the Key and Quill Shop with its interesting variety of 18th-century reproductions, including furniture, accessories and maps.

Just a few steps away is Independence National Historical Park with its 12 acres of lawn in the heart of the city, 31 buildings, courtyards and a variety of cafes, some with alfresco dining.

Details

Check in: 1 p.m. Check out: 11 a.m. Deposit/Cancellation Policy: reservations guaranteed with credit card, refunded with 48 hours' notice. Payment: cash, personal check, MasterCard, VISA, American Express. Children welcome. Smoking is permitted, but no cigars or pipes. Unsuitable for guest pets. Kennels nearby. First floor rear access is handicap accessible. Central air conditioning. Parking in municipal parking garage adjacent to inn.

Rates

$80 - $150 double occupancy. $150 suites. $15 extra person in room. Valet service available for additional charge. Best to call several weeks in advance for major weekends.

Bed & Bath

Ten 18th-century guest rooms with the look and feel of a colonial Williamsburg inn, and two spacious suites with gas log fireplaces, writing desks, whirlpool/shower combination and queen-size poster beds. All rooms contain twin, double, or queen-size beds, televisions, telephones, alarm clocks and period furnishings that reflect the rooms' original occupants. The top floors were originally the servants' quarters and are, therefore, furnished with wrought iron or pine headboards, whereas the lower floor rooms feature cherry furnishings and four-poster beds reflecting the status and wealth of the gentry.

Breakfast & Extras

Served in an intimate dining room, a filling breakfast featuring quiche, bacon or sausage, fruit garnish, freshly baked muffins and breads, and beverages. Afternoon tea and biscuits available for guests upon request. Evening wine and cheese served in the candlelit dining room.

Extra Facilities & Features

Space available for conferences, wedding receptions, and special gatherings up to 30 people. Catering can be arranged for lunches and dinners. Special corporate discount. Ask about packaged weekend activities including murder mystery weekends and gourmet cooking demonstrations.

Jerry & Lisa Dunn,
Innkeepers

129 S. Second St., Philadelphia, PA 19106. Phone: (215) 923-8523 or (800) 845-BOND (2663), Monday - Friday 9 a.m. to 3 p.m., answering machine other times. Location: Philadelphia County, in Olde City Philadelphia in Society Hill between Chestnut and Walnut Streets, within Independence National Historic Park.

WEDGWOOD
COLLECTION
OF INNS

ne enters the drive at the Wedgwood over the same road that was used 200 years ago by General Alexander Lord Stirling during the Revolutionary War. The present structure was built on the stone foundations of an earlier colonial house. Lord Stirling stayed in the earlier house during an encampment in December 1776 prior to George Washington's famous crossing of the Delaware.

One of three historic 19th-century properties in the Wedgwood Collection, the Wedgwood is a gracious 1870 Victorian, while the adjacent Umpleby House is a Classic Revival stone manor circa 1833. The most recent addition to the group is the Aaron Burr House, built in 1854 by the same person who built Wedgwood three doors down the street.

Hardwood floors, lofty windows and antique furnishings recreate a warm, comfortable 19th-century aura. In addition, Carl and Nadine have carefully appointed each inn with original art, handmade quilts and Wedgwood pottery, particularly prevalent at the Wedgwood House.

Two acres of gardens, brick walkways and well-tended grounds adjoin the Umpleby House and Wedgwood. A gazebo with veranda porch offers quiet space to relax after a busy day, while the hammock beckons folks desiring an afternoon snooze.

All three properties offer an ideal "home base" for leisurely strolls within this square-mile community. Visitors will find a myriad of boutiques, craft and antique shops, art galleries and restaurants, all built around three centuries of classic architecture in a village founded in 1681.

Details

Check in: 2 p.m. Check out: 11 a.m. Deposit/Cancellation Policy: 50% sent, 10-day notice required for full refund, if less and if room is rebooked, $15 service charge. Payment: cash or personal check preferred. American Express accepted for business accounts. Limited accommodations for children and pets, inquire upon making reservation. Smoking outside only. In residence: brown labrador, Jasper. All rooms are air conditioned, most have ceiling fans. Limited handicap access. Off-street parking.

Rates

$70 - $125 double occupancy. Suites $125 - $160. Carriage House $160. $20 for additional person in room. Two-night minimum stay weekends, three-night minimum stay holiday weekends. Best to call one month in advance.

Bed & Bath

Eighteen rooms and suites at three separate properties. The Aaron Burr House has six rooms with private baths and queen or king-size beds. Both the Umpleby House and the adjacent Wedgwood House have six rooms with double and queen-size beds, private and semi-private baths. Furnished with Victorian antiques from local antique shops and flea markets. Toiletries in baths, fresh flowers in rooms, Amish quilts on most beds. At day's end, guests will find a tot of homemade liqueur bedside, mints on pillows and bed covers turned down.

Breakfast & Extras

Depending upon property and season, breakfast may be served in gazebo or sunporch, fireside in formal dining room, or in privacy of guest room. A continental-plus breakfast that includes ricotta-pineapple poppy-seed muffins, fresh fruit, yogurt, juice and beverages. Saturday afternoon sweet tea is served with Dinie's famous Swedish apple pie, a favorite.

Extra Facilities & Features

Three conference parlors available for small business meetings and retreats. Corporate rate and long-term relocation rates upon request. Fax available. Call or write about innkeeping seminars, apprenticeships and consultations. Arrangements may be made with advance notice for a moonlight carriage ride to a local restaurant or theater and return ride to inn.

Carl Glassman & Nadine Silnutzer

111 W. Bridge St., New Hope, PA 18938. Phone: (215) 862-2570, best to call 10 a.m. to 10 p.m., answering machine other times. Location: Bucks County, all three inns are located in the heart of New Hope's historic district.

WHITEHALL

The year is 1840 and the courier has just delivered a formal invitation for an afternoon tea. An invitation this coveted comes all too rarely. With tea being so precious, it is kept under lock and key. Servants even suspected of stealing tea are summarily dismissed. The English social event of high tea is reserved for the wealthy and prominent. On this day, the hostess has also managed to secure another, equally-prized commodity: sugar, ensuring that sweets will accompany her tea and that she will bestow the ultimate gesture of hospitality upon her guests.

Although sugar and tea are commonplace now, what is not is the English tradition of high tea. One hundred and fifty years later, Whitehall Inn continues this hallmark of British hospitality. Each day, precisely at 4 p.m., new arrivals and current guests can be found in the parlor or sun room, sipping perfectly-brewed tea and sampling an afternoon repast that would be the envy of any 19th-century hostess. With chamber music playing in the background, guests relax after a busy day.

Mike and Suella found this circa-1794 plantation manor on 13 acres of countryside in 1985 and proceeded to create the inn of their dreams. If success is measured in accolades and awards, they have succeeded beyond even their high expectations. Suella's cuisine has been applauded in gourmet magazines across the country. The romantic atmosphere is carefully nurtured even to the inclusion of live chamber music provided by musicians invited to perform at the inn.

In the morning, after a breakfast that defies definition, perhaps the best revelation is that it didn't take an invitation delivered by courier to experience Whitehall.

Details

Check in: 3 - 7 p.m. Check out: 11 a.m. Deposit/Cancellation Policy: one night's stay sent or credit card guarantee; refunded less $25 handling charge with 31 days' notice when cancelling or shortening reservation. Payment: cash, personal check, MasterCard, VISA, American Express, Diners Club, Discover, or Carte Blanche. Children over 12 welcome. No smoking inside inn or on grounds. Limited handicap access first floor rooms. Guest rooms air conditioned. Unsuitable for guest pets. Kennels nearby. Off-street parking.

Rates

$120 - $170 double occupancy. Suite: $170. Two-night minimum weekends, three-night minimum holidays. Best to call eight weeks in advance for peak times.

Bed & Bath

Six guest rooms, four with private baths, working fireplaces, all named for prior owners. Located on three floors, rooms contain period antiques, queen or double beds, numerous special touches that contribute to the romantic aura permeating each room. A bottle of Bucks County wine, crystal wine and tumbler glasses, fresh flowers, Evelyn and Crabtree toiletries, Whitehall's own rose potpourri and bath salts, and velour robes are just a few of the extras guests can expect to find in their rooms.

Breakfast & Extras

Served in formal dining room with its expansive picture window, overlooking open fields and horse pastures, a four-course breakfast that takes 1 1/2 to two hours to experience and was once declared "sumptuous" by **Bon Appetit** magazine. The pervasive use of candlelight, heirloom sterling, fresh flowers, European crystal and china atop a white linen set table evokes an elegant atmosphere uncommon for dinner, unheard of for breakfast. A typical feast opens with Whitehall's secret blend coffee, English and herbal teas, and freshly squeezed honey tangerine juice. The bread may include Suella's prize-winning butter coffee cake and maple cream biscuits. The next course could be Apple Sweet Paprika soup followed by cinnamon-crusted baked pears with cognac custard sauce. The main course may feature spinach tarts with toasted pine nuts and Parmesan cheese. Whitehall chocolates and jarlsberg cheese are the finale. High tea at 4 p.m. includes a perfectly brewed pot of tea accompanied by an assortment of finger sandwiches, sweets, scones, Devonshire

cream and preserves. Evening sherry is served fireside in the parlor. Whitehall chocolates found bedside.

Extra Facilities & Features

Space available for small business meetings up to 12. Fax available. Catering for lunch and dinner possible. Special corporate rate. On-site in-ground pool, badminton and tennis courts. Dressage horses graze the pastures, and like an occasional carrot and pat on the nose. Inquire about theme weekends that include the popular Chocolate Lovers Get Away.

Mike & Suella Wass

R. D. #2, Box 250 (1370 Pineville Road),
New Hope, PA 18939. Phone: (215) 598-
7945, 10 a.m. - 10 p.m., answering machine
on occasion. Location: Bucks County,
Route 202 South, left on Street Road, then
right on Pineville, 1 1/2 miles ahead on
right. About 4 miles from historic New
Hope, 2 miles from Peddlers Village.

YE OLDE TEMPERANCE HOUSE

$\mathcal{I}$t's not hard to imagine Newtown serving as a busy county seat in the mid 1700s - early 1800s, with its horse-drawn carriages ushering travelers to their lodging destinations. Carriages loaded with passengers would pull up to a hostelry's platform, allowing passengers to disembark without having to step down to street level. The Temp's platform still stands today, testimony to the changes this 18th-century inn has witnessed.

Built in 1772, this lovely three-story brick and stone colonial combines rural charm and city style in a setting that caters to guests' lodging, food, and entertainment needs with an attentive staff that goes out of its way to offer personalized service.

The guest rooms situated on the front side of the inn enjoy a view of Bucks County's rolling farmlands. Sleeping quarters on the far side face historic Court Street where quaint brownstones dating back to colonial times line the narrow thoroughfare.

The turn-of-the-century lobby acts as a gateway to the Tavern, four dining rooms and a banquet room. Food and drink are offered in a warm and friendly atmosphere.

Live jazz Wednesday through Sunday brings a bit of New Orleans and Mardi Gras to quiet Bucks County. On weekends there is lively entertainment with Friday evenings featuring the Twilight Jamboree and Saturday evenings a well-known guest performer. On Sundays a Dixieland Jazz Brunch takes place, making a weekend visit to the Temp one that guests will not soon forget.

Details

Check in: 2 p.m. Check out: 12 p.m. Deposit/Cancellation Policy: one-night's deposit or credit card guarantee. 24 hours notice for cancellations. Payment: cash, MasterCard, VISA, American Express, or Diners Club. Children welcome. Smoking permitted. Unsuitable for guest pets, but kennels nearby. No handicap access. Central air conditioning. Television in guest rooms. Off-street parking.

Rates

$95 - $135 double occupancy (except Leedom Room - rate includes up to four persons). $15 for cot. Best to call one month in advance for major weekends. Valet and laundry services extra.

Bed & Bath

Ten rooms and three suites, all with private baths. Bed range in size from double to king. The Leedom Room has two double beds. The Hicks Suite has working fireplace and king-size bed. The Benetz Suite has unusual bent hickory and willow twig furniture with a king-size bed. All rooms have 18th and 19th-century furnishings. Many have stenciled walls and handcut and handpainted lamp shades. All named for a special period or person in the inn's history.

Breakfast & Extras

Served in Breakfast Room, Monday through Saturday: freshly baked muffins, fresh fruit, juice and coffee. Special Sunday Dixieland Jazz Brunch from 11 a.m. - 3 p.m., with music from 1 - 5 p.m. Evening dining for every mood in one of four dining areas, each separately decorated and appointed. From a picturesque Victorian setting in the William R. Hallowell Dining Room to the colonial atmosphere in the Edward Hicks Dining Room with its open hearths, handpainted murals. The diners for lunch and dinner will enjoy a wide array of temptations including fresh seafood, beef and poultry, as well as Rack of Lamb and veal prepared to order.

Extra Facilities & Features

Space available for conferences and banquets for up to 100 attendees. Corporate rate available. Getaway packages. Overnight guests have use of racquetball and fitness clubs 1 3/10-miles from inn.

Jim Calderone

5-11 S. State St., Newtown, PA 18940. Phone: (215) 860-0474, 24 hours a day. Fax: (215) 321-7152. Location: Bucks County, off Route 95 at Newtown exit, Route 332 west to sixth light, on South State Street, turn left.

BISCHWIND

Barbara Von Dran

Route 115, Box 7, Bear Creek, PA 18602. Phone: (717) 472-3820 or 735-2114, anytime. Location: Luzerne County, off North East Extension (Route 9) Exit 36, south 3 miles on Route 115. 20 minutes from I-80 and I-81.

POCONO MOUNTAINS

lbert Lewis, lumber and ice baron, built his 32-room English manor in 1883. This imposing structure dominates eight groomed acres of lawn and woods. The estate contains nine baths, nine fireplaces, a crystal drawing room measuring 45 feet by 28 feet, and rooms filled with antiques, many original to the mansion.

The expansive grounds include trails for skiing, hiking, biking and horseback riding. There are two dressage courts, a pond, plus an in-ground pool.

The Von Drans' hobby is raising and showing Trakehner horses and driving carriages, an interest reflected in the unique collection of horse-related items found throughout the home.

While visiting the Von Drans, guests are welcome to relax in the parlor with its 100-year-old Steinway grand piano and have afternoon tea and cakes.

Details

Flexible check in. Check out: 6 p.m. Deposit/Cancellation Policy: payment in advance, refunded with seven days' notice. Payment: personal check, MasterCard, VISA, Discover. Children over 12 welcome. No smoking inside. Unsuitable for guest pets. Kennels nearby. In residence: school-age son, Eric; three cats. Cool, wooded setting; no air conditioning needed. No handicap access. Off-street parking.

Rates

$150 - $250 double occupancy.

Bed & Bath

Three areas. The guest cottage, Doll House, has kitchen, bath and living room; Bridal Suite has queen-size Victorian bed, fireplace, living room, and bath with antique, oversize tub. Blue Room has double bed and private bath.

Breakfast & Extras

Served in formal English dining room or on terrace, a breakfast planned around each guest's palate. A typical menu may include filet mignon with mushrooms, quiche, eggs to order, sparkling fruit juice, fruit platter, muffins and beverages. Coffee and dessert available most afternoons. Early morning coffee tray offered.

Extra Facilities & Features

Space available for up to six for small meetings and conferences. Catering can be arranged. Special corporate rate. Many on-site recreational activities.

ACADEMY STREET BED & BREAKFAST

Civil War hero Captain Joseph Atkinson chose the little village of Hawley to begin his new civilian life. His involvement in the local lumber trade is reflected throughout the home.

Choosing a site atop a hill near the Lackawaxen River, he proceeded to build one of the finest homes in Hawley. Built in 1863, his Italianate Victorian mansion boasted cherry wood floors, mahogany doors, oversized windows, fine millwork and cabinetry, plaster moldings, custom glass works, and high ceilings.

One of the few homes not to be washed away during the "great flood," it fell into disrepair and obscurity during the 20th-century. Rescued by a commercial artist, the home had already undergone substantial restoration when Judith happened upon it.

A trip to Europe inspired her to open an inn, and the home at 528 Academy Street fulfilled that dream.

Today guests are hard-pressed to decide what it is about Academy Street Bed & Breakfast they like most: the attractive comfortable rooms with their eclectic mixture of Victorian antiques and collection of vintage movie star photos, or Judith herself, with her delightful sense of humor and easygoing personality.

Details

Check in: anytime. Check out: 11 a.m. Deposit/Cancellation Policy: no deposit necessary, appreciate 24 hours' notice of cancellation. Payment: cash, MasterCard, or VISA. Children 14 and older welcome. Smoking is permitted. Unsuitable for guest pets. No handicap access. Guest rooms air conditioned. Off-street parking.

Rates

$75 double occupancy. $30 for additional person in room. Best to call four weeks in advance during peak times. Two-night minimum on holiday weekends.

Bed & Bath

Six guest rooms, three with private bath in room, one with half bath in room, shares full hall bath with two other rooms. Captains Room and Sun Room have one double bed; Elizabeth Browning Room, Jane Eyre Room, and Country Room have queen-size bed. The Victorian Room has two twins.

Breakfast & Extras

Served in formal dining room, a gourmet buffet on weekends that features spinach pie, amaretta French toast, Mediterranean egg tarts, muffins, breads, fruit, juice and beverages. Through the week a continental breakfast is served. During summer months guests enjoy afternoon tea on large front porch, sampling some of Judith's delectable homebaked pastries and cakes. Upon retiring, guests will find next to the bed another plate of Judith's ever-present sweets for late night snacks.

Judith & Sheldon Lazan

528 Academy St., Hawley, PA 18428. Phone: (717) 226-3430, best to call during the day, evenings leave message on machine. Open May 30 to October 30. During winter months call: (201) 316-8148 or write 53 Lake Shore Drive, Lake Hiawatha, NJ 07034. Location: Wayne County, I-84 Exit 8 North, Route 6 West to Hawley and Lake Wallenpaupack resort area.

BEACH LAKE
HOTEL

$\mathfrak{I}$f walls could talk, those in the Beach Lake Hotel would have more than their share of tales to recount.

Records indicate that this 1830s building has been welcoming the public in one capacity or another for over 150 years. A one-time stopover for tired and hungry travelers, it has also been a general store and served as a United States post office from 1879 to 1936. During 1897 a major renovation was undertaken, and 90 years later the Millers did it again.

The building was called the Beach Lake Hotel during the Civil War, and the Millers reclaimed the name when opening their hostelry. After a year of extensive restoration that included retaining old walls and woodwork when possible and carefully reproducing when necessary, they opened an elegant country inn reminiscent of an earlier era.

Inveterate inn travelers themselves, they knew it took more than a pretty building to create a successful inn. Erika's culinary talents, Roy's wry sense of humor (ask to read one of his newsletters) and their enjoyment of people bring guests back to Beach Lake Hotel.

The inn is located in the quiet greenbelt area of the Pocono Mountains, renowned for the scenic backroads, mountain-fed lakes, and sleepy hamlets. Just a short drive away is a variety of area landmarks, including the Stourbridge Lion in Honesdale, a replica of America's first locomotive. A 4 1/2- hour excursion along the Laxawaxen River includes two stops, one at the Zane Grey Museum and the other at the Roebling Bridge, designed by the architect of the Brooklyn Bridge.

Details

Check in: 12 noon. Check out: 11 a.m. Deposit/Cancellation Policy: prepayment of one-night's stay. Refunded with ten days' notice prior to date of reservation or if room is rebooked. Payment: cash, personal check, MasterCard, VISA, or American Express. Unsuitable for children. No guest pets. Kennels nearby. Smoking permitted in common areas only, no cigars or pipes. In residence: shi-tsu dog, Abbigail. No handicap access. Individually controlled air conditioning units in guest rooms and dining rooms. Off-street parking.

Rates

$85 double occupancy. $25 for roll-away. Two-night minimum stay on holidays and June through October weekends. Best to call one month in advance for peak times.

Bed & Bath

Six guest rooms with private baths, tastefully decorated with different color schemes, using authentic Victorian wall papers and imported lace. All furnished with Victorian-era antiques, comfortable chairs, a mini-library, and antique double beds. Toiletries provided in bath, fruit bowls in room. Several rooms share a common balcony, complete with rocking chairs for a late-night session of stargazing. Nearly all antique furnishings and appointments are for sale, acquisitions from Roy and Erika's frequent trips to estate sales, auctions and antique shops.

Breakfast & Extras

Served in the formal dining room, a country breakfast that features such fare as eggs benedict or apple pancakes, always a fresh-baked surprise, accompanied by a breakfast meat and juice, beverages. Erika's cookies are available for snacking anytime. The cozy Pub offers a genteel social setting for a pre-dinner cocktail or an after-dinner cordial, while the television keeps news addicts in touch with the outside world. Candlelight dinners are open to both guests and the public. Dinner reservations are best made the same time as room reservations since Erika's reputation for creating flavorful dishes is known throughout the region. Entrees may include quail in Cognac sauce or sauteed veal topped with olives and tomatoes. Desserts like mocha cheese cake with raspberry sauce provide the calorie-laden conclusion to a memorable dinner — but who's counting?

Extra Facilities & Features

Conference space for up to 30 participants. Special corporate rate. Wedding receptions for up to 50 in restaurant. The backyard orchard and garden yield a veritable produce market of fruits and vegetables. Fishing and swimming in adjacent Beach Lake. The Gallery features antique furnishings, old oil paintings and unique collectibles.

Erika & Roy Miller

Box 144, Main Street and Church Road, Beach Lake, PA 18405. Phone: (717) 729-8239, from 9 a.m. to 9 p.m., answering machine other times, restaurant closed Tuesday and Wednesday. Location: Wayne County, 4 miles from the Delaware River, 1/2 mile off Route 652 in village of Beach Lake.

BLACK WALNUT INN

Hidden away on a 160-acre estate, 1 1/2- miles from the main road, is this 1940s English Tudor-style stone home with its wrap-around porch and rustic, tranquil setting.

As guests approach, they are greeted by the Schneiders' friendly retriever, Rex. The warm and comfortable atmosphere is not unlike that of visiting old friends and favored relatives.

Guests are encouraged to make use of all the many facilities Stewart has provided for his guests. His goal is to offer folks an unpretentious place where they can meet other people who just want to get away.

Close by are the famous Delaware Water Gap, with canoeing and rafting, and Bushkill Falls, a 300-acre natural park. Historic sites include Grey Towers and the Hiawatha Stagecoach, both in Milford. Also nearby are riding stables. But with the long list of indoor and outdoor recreational facilities that the Schneiders have provided for their guests, many folks never have the time to leave this secluded estate.

The outdoor enthusiast can enjoy the inn's paddleboats and swimming docks on the four-acre pond. Fishing, hiking and cross-country skiing give guest a chance to view the wildlife that inhabitsthe 160 acres of woods and fields.

Other pastimes include napping in the hammock, soaking in the hot tub, playing pool or pingpong, and pitching horseshoes.

Details

Check in: 3 p.m. Check out: 11 a.m. Deposit/Cancellation Policy: 50% deposit upon making reservation; cancellation credit issued good for one year. Payment: cash, personal check, MasterCard, VISA, or American Express. Children welcome. Smoking in designated areas only. Unsuitable for guest pets. In residence: Labrador retrievers, Rex and Bear. No handicap access. No air conditioning. Off-street parking.

Rates

$60 - $85 double occupancy. Children's sleeping bags permitted. Best to call one month in advance for holiday weekends. Two-night minimum these weekends.

Bed & Bath

Twelve guest rooms. Four with full bath in room, four with one-half bath in room, and four share two hallway baths. Queen and double-size antique and brass beds.

Breakfast & Extras

Served in large dining room at individual tables, with full-length picture windows overlooking a large pond, a buffet-style breakfast that includes cereal, eggs, bacon, fruit salad, bagels, lox, cream cheese, freshly baked breads and streusels, homemade preserves and beverages. Iced tea served on summer afternoons, dessert and coffee on weekend evenings. Sherry is offered evenings by the fireplace.

Extra Features & Facilities

Meeting space available for small corporate retreats up to 24 persons and weddings up to 100 persons. Catered lunch and dinner can be arranged. There is a piano and a VCR with video library. The barbecue grill on the porch is for guests' use plus kids delight in visiting the petting zoo. Innkeeper Hermien is from the Netherlands, speaks fluent Dutch, and has a penchant for making sure everything is sparkling clean.

Hermien Ankersmith,
Innkeeper
Stewart & Effie Schneider,
Owners

Fire Tower Road., R. D. #2, Box 9285, Milford, PA 18337. Phone: (717) 296-6322, anytime. Location: Pike County, 2 miles off I-84 Exit 10.

INN AT MEADOWBROOK

Secluded on 43 idyllic acres of flowers, woods and meadows, Meadowbrook takes its name from the large fishing pond that overflows into a crystal-clear brook and meadow.

Built in the mid-1800s by a family who helped settle the area, the small farmhouse was expanded over the generations. In 1940 the new owners added a horse stable and indoor arena and opened Meadowbrook as a riding farm. Guests visiting today can still enjoy the equestrian sport.

Across the road, the Mill House has been restored into a second guest area and is the location of the old gristmill.

At the Manor House, the dining room opens out onto a large deck and terrace, overlooking the gazebo at pond's edge — a picture-book setting for an outdoor wedding.

Inside there are two common rooms to meet every guest's needs. The first-floor formal living room with its fireplace offers a quiet place to read while the lower level "rec" room has a variety of games and activities.

In warm months, the English garden beds and flower pots add summer color to the swimming pool and wicker-filled pool house.

All the outdoor activities available at Meadowbrook make it easy to forget the inn is located in the heart of the Pocono Mountains, only minutes away from major ski areas, mountain lakes and state parks.

Details

Check in: 2 p.m. Check out: 12 noon. Deposit/Cancellation Policy: one night's deposit, refunded with seven days' notice prior to reservations. Payment: cash, personal check, MasterCard, VISA, or American Express. Children over 11 welcome. Smoking permitted in designated areas. Unsuitable for guest pets. Kennels nearby. No handicap access. No air conditioning, but window fans available. Off-street parking.

Rates

$50 - $85 double occupancy. Best to call two months in advance for peak weekends and holidays. Two-night minimum stay on weekends.

Bed & Bath

The 16 rooms are located in two separate areas. The Manor House has five large rooms with private baths and six smaller rooms with sinks in room, sharing two hallway baths. The Mill House is a small guest house with five rooms and private baths, a commons room called the Stone Room, the former location of the old gristmill. Beds are queen- or double-size and furnishings are an eclectic mixture of antiques, wicker and contemporary. The Pink Room, used as a Bridal Suite, is also a favorite Manor House Room for special occasions, while the Log Room with its trompe l'oeil logs painted on the whitewash walls is the favored room in the Mill House.

Breakfast & Extras

Served in formal dining room with its pretty view of gazebo, a buffet breakfast featuring blueberry pancakes, French toast, bacon or sausage, cereal, freshly baked muffins and breads, juice and beverages. Hall refrigerator is filled with complimentary soft drinks and juices. Evening dining available Tuesday through Saturday. Advance reservations required. Additional charge. In warmer months, late afternoon refreshments are served on the deck overlooking the terraced lawn, brook and pond.

Extra Facilities & Features

Space available for business meetings and receptions up to 50 persons. Catering for lunch and dinner available. Special corporate rate. On-site pool, badminton, volleyball and tennis courts, hiking trails, fishing and horses — stables available for guests' horses. The lower level "rec" room has a fieldstone fireplace, game tables, television, piano and wet bar.

Bob & Kathy Overman

R. D. #7, Box 7651, East Stroudsburg, PA 18301. Phone: (717) 629-0296, best to call 9 a.m. - 10 p.m., answering machine other times. Location: Monroe County, off I-80 Exit 45, 1 mile south on Route 611, left onto Cherry Lane Road then 5 miles.

INN AT STARLIGHT LAKE

Back when pocket watches were an instrument for marking time rather than a man's ornament, and when parasols, not umbrellas, were de rigueur for fashionable ladies, the Starlight Inn welcomed its first guests.

Since 1909, when the inn opened its doors, it has continued to be a place where visitors can relax and renew themselves. Hospitality and courteous treatment, hallmarks of the inn's early existence, continue through the personable nature of innkeepers, Jack and Judy McMahon.

The inn is located beside Starlight Lake, known for its crystal-clear, mountain-fed spring water. Acres of untouched forests and farmland meadows surround the quaint turn-of-the-century inn. Fern banks, moss-covered boulders, shady dells and natural woodland scenes greet the eye at every turn.

The year-round country inn offers activities for every season. Spring opens with canoeing, rowing and sailing. The lake is ideal for a hot summer's day dip. Fall brings a myriad of colors from mid-September to mid-October, while 18 miles of wooded trails and gentle slopes will challenge even the most ardent cross-country skiers during winter months.

The relaxed, comfortable atmosphere of the common room, with its toasty, wood-burning fire for warming frosty toes, and the variety of board games, is sure to keep everyone from the young to the young-at-heart entertained on rainy days and quiet evenings.

Details

Check in: 1 p.m. Check out: 12 noon. Deposit/Cancellation Policy: one night deposit, refunded with ten days' notice prior to date. Payment: cash, personal check, MasterCard, or VISA. Children welcome. Smoking permitted in designated areas. Unsuitable for guest pets, kennel nearby. In residence, a golden retriever, Chelsea. No handicap access. Ceiling and window fans in rooms. Off-street parking.

Rates

$110 - $140 double occupancy. $170 - $185 suites. $49 for third person in room. Children under seven free in same room with parents. Food charged a la cart. Children 7 through 12, $37 each, same room with parents. Rates include an allotment of $10 for breakfast and $40 for dinner, per couple. Child's allotment is $2.50 and $8.50 each. Best to call two months in advance for peak times. Two-night minimum stay summer, winter, Fall Foliage (October), and holiday weekends.

Bed & Bath

There are five distinct properties including the Main House with 14 rooms, decorated to represent the early 1900s period. Next to it is the two-bedroom Hillside Cottage with a porch overlooking the lake and popular with families. The Skylight Cottage, behind the tennis court, has three rooms, each with bath and opening onto a long porch overlooking the lake. The Lakeside Cottage is a three-level building with four units, all with porches overlooking the lake. Inside, there is the Suite with king-size bed, whirlpool, and bidet; the Fireplace Room connects with another room, and Tree Tops features two sleeping alcoves children love. The Annex House is a three-bedroom split-level house that can sleep up to 12, popular for family reunions. All facilities are furnished and appointed with selections that include "finds" from Grandmom's attic to modern furniture with clean simple lines.

rooms. For a late-night snack and night cap, the Stovepipe Bar offers a congenial setting.

Breakfast & Extras

Served in the pleasant informality of lakeside dining, open to the public, diners can choose from varied breakfast, lunch, and dinner menus sure to please any palate. Rates for inn guests include an allotment for breakfast and dinner. Picnic lunches, for an additional charge, can be prepared. Homebaked bread is served at every meal. Upon arrival, guests will find a welcoming bowl of fresh fruit in their

Extra Facilities & Features

Conference space for up to 20. Restaurant open to the public. Special corporate rate. On-site recreation includes swimming, boating, canoeing and fishing. Tennis courts, shuffleboard, and bicycles available. Inn owns a small fleet of canoes, rowboats, and sailboats for guest use. There are 18 miles of marked and groomed trails for cross-country skiers. Ski equipment rentals and professional instruction available.

Jack & Judy McMahon

P.O. Box 27, Starlight, PA 18847. Phone: (717) 798-2519, 8 a.m. - 10 p.m., answering machine other times. Location: Wayne County, 5 miles south of Route 17 at Hancock, New York; 30 miles from I-81 Exit 62.

PONDA-ROWLAND BED & BREAKFAST

ost bed and breakfasts have some kind of trademark amenity or unique feature; however, few include a pair of binoculars.

Here, as evening approaches, the ponds and fields fill up with Canadian geese, whitetail deer, and mallard ducks coming in to feed. For most folks, just relaxing on the enclosed porch, enjoying the panoramic view of the mountainside would be enough, but with the binoculars, a close-up view of native wildlife becomes a special treat.

The Rowland family has established a 30-acre wildlife sanctuary complete with trails, ponds and feeding stations. Guests are delighted at the menagerie of creatures frequenting the property. Majestic blue herons, snow geese, and even an old squaw duck make appearances. Guests witness such scenes as a mallard hen parading her ten chicks around the pond while mature deer bring their fawns to play and feed. While hiking, guests will often catch sight of a fox, flock of turkeys, or even a bear.

Located in the Endless Mountain region of northern Pennsylvania, this 1850s plank farmhouse is a showpiece of American antiques. The array of primitive furnishings includes collections of crocks, pewter, tools and coffee grinders, all museum quality. Recent additions showcase the Rowland son's mastery of timber framing. The B & B proves to be an ideal place for everyone from business travelers seeking a secure and quiet location to families longing for a farm vacation experience.

Details

Check in and check out: flexible.
Deposit/Cancellation Policy: one-night's lodging deposit, two weeks' notice, less a $5 service charge, for cancellations. Payment: cash, personal check, MasterCard, or VISA. All children welcome. No smoking inside. No pets in guest rooms. No handicap access. No air conditioning; rooms have ceiling fans. Parking at door.

Rates

$50 - $60 double occupancy. No charge for one child in room. Best to reserve two weeks ahead for holiday weekends. 30% discount for stays exceeding three days during the week.

Bed & Bath

Three guest rooms each with private bath. Amish Room has two twin cannonball beds, 18th century amoire, and fantastic view of wildlife sanctuary. King Room has king-size bed (or alternatively, two twins) and the same view. Maple Room, overlooking the farm fields, has double bed and dresser in birdseye maple.

Breakfast & Extras

Depending upon season, served in the dining room by candlelight on a long chestnut farmer's table, the enclosed porch, or fireside in the Great Room. Full country breakfast includes pancakes, French toast, eggs, cereals, toast, jellies, fruit platter, juice and beverages. Can arrange vegetarian or special diets. Full view of the wildlife sanctuary wherever breakfast served. Afternoon beverages available. Popcorn by the fireplace offered at night.

Extra Facilities & Features

On-sight toboggan, hiking, and cross-country ski trails. Five ponds for fishing, swimming and ice skating. Canoe available. Ask in advance about hay rides. Satellite television brings 96 channels including HBO and Disney.

Jeanette & Cliff Rowland

R. D. #1, Box 349, Dallas, PA 18612. Phone: (717) 639-3245, best to call early morning or mid-evening, answering machine other times. Location: Wyoming County, 1/2 mile off Route 309, at the end of the paved road and on a 130-acre farm, 4 miles north of Dallas, 12 miles south of Tunkhannock in the Village of Beaumont.

SETTLERS INN

ocated in the Lake Region of the Poconos, the Settlers Inn stands not only as a monument to the grand hotels of the 1920s but as an example of what can be accomplished by a small town with community spirit. The people of Hawley, foreseeing the emergence of a tourist industry with the formation of Lake Wallenpaupack, began construction of this formal English Tudor mansion in 1927.

Efforts were stalled through the Great Depression and World War II, but since the mansion's completion, the building has been home to a hotel, a school for boys, a nightclub and a haven for the elderly. In 1980, the present owners purchased it and have built it into an inn where the atmosphere of friendliness is so pervasive visitors claim that "even the flowers out front greet summer arrivals."

One reason for the Settlers Inn's success not only with overnight guests but with local patrons is the excellent fare offered in the public dining room.

The owner, who is also the chef, takes special pride in preparing cuisine based on regional food traditions and locally-produced ingredients. Fish and game come from nearby farms and the organic fruits and vegetables are locally grown. The inn cures and smokes its own meats and its gardens produce most of the herbs used in cooking. The result is an enjoyable dining experience not soon forgotten.

Details

Check in: after 1:00 p.m. Check out: noon. Deposit/Cancellation Policy: credit card guarantee or one night's lodging in advance. Refund sent with three days' notice.

Payment: cash, personal check, MasterCard, VISA, or American Express. All well-behaved children welcome. Smoking permitted in designated areas. Unsuitable for guest pets. The dining room is handicap accessible. Air conditioning in all guest rooms, dining room, and public rooms, but not in hallways. Off-street parking.

Rates

$65 - $80 double occupancy. $100 - $120 suites (all with private bath). $15 for extra person in room. Children permitted to bring own sleeping bag with advance notice, extra person rate applies. Best to make reservations for holidays and weekends four weeks in advance.

Bed & Bath

Twelve guest rooms plus three suites of two rooms each, all with private bath. All individually decorated with a simple mixture of "early attic" antiques, family heirlooms, and post-'40s furnishings. One double bed in each room; suites have either two double beds or one double and two twins. Also, two upstairs sitting rooms where guests can socialize.

Breakfast & Extras

Served in downstairs dining room; a choice of cornmeal pancakes, eggs, homemade granola, sweet breads, fruit and beverages. Warm afternoons guests can relax on the airy front porch with a cold drink. Evenings in the Tavern, a selection of Pennsylvania-made cheeses and homemade breads and crackers can be found for guest to nibble on while enjoying fellowship around the massive stone fireplace.

Extra Facilities & Features

Besides the main dining room, there are several smaller dining rooms for business meetings and family parties. Also facilities to accommodate up to 120 persons for wedding receptions, business conferences and under-tent garden parties. Special holiday event packages available. Phone jacks available for all guest rooms. Inquire about special corporate rate.

Across the street is a large park with tennis and basketball courts. Lake Wallenpaupack with all of its diverse recreational facilities is just two miles away.

Marcia Dunsmore, *Innkeeper*
Jeanne & Grant Genzlinger,
Owners

4 Main St., Hawley, PA 18428. Phone: (717) 226-2993, best to call between 8 a.m. and 10 p.m. Location: Wayne County, follow I-84 to Exit 6, north on Route 507 to Route 6 West, 1 1/2 miles, just outside of downtown Hawley.

BED & BREAKFAST CONNECTIONS RSO

Miller House

For reservations, contact Bed & Breakfast Connections, Box 21, Devon, PA 19333. Phone: (215) 687-3565 or (800) 448-3619 (outside PA), 9 a.m. - 9 p.m., Monday - Saturday, 1 - 9 p.m., Sunday, answering machine other times. Location: York County, 15 miles southeast of York outside the village of Brogue.

nce owned by Benjamin Franklin's grandson, this magnificent Susquehanna River estate was built in 1740 atop a hill. Below is a restored late-1800s guest cottage, nestled in the woods alongside a meandering stream. Its screened-in porch offers a relaxing place to enjoy the quiet of the woods, the babbling of the creek, and the rustling of the wind through the leaves.

Miller House is perfect for families or three couples traveling together. The youngsters can take a dip in the old-fashioned swimming hole, while Mom and Dad drop a line in the stream. There is an old gristmill to explore and trails for hiking and biking.

With its large, fully equipped kitchen, sunny dining room and living room, this charming cottage is an ideal base for visiting Historic York and all of south central Pennsylvania's attractions. Boating on the Susquehanna is a mile away, and fine restaurants and a winery are nearby.

Details

Check in and out: noon. Deposit/Cancellation Policy: one night handling fee plus tax. Refunded, less a $15 service charge if cancellation is seven days or more prior to arrival date. Payment: personal check, MasterCard, VISA, American Express. Children welcome. Smoking in designated areas. No handicap access. Guest pets are permitted. Central air conditioning.

Rates

$75 per night for two. Family of four-$90. Only one group up to six people may book cottage at one time.

Bed & Bath

Cottage has three attractively decorated rooms, each with delicate selection of pastels on white creating a bright, cheerful atmosphere. Modern bath, king, double, and twin-bedded rooms.

Breakfast & Extras

Choice of full breakfast in the 1740s main house or a continental breakfast delivered to cottage where the sunny dining room affords view of woods. At special request, host will stock cottage refrigerator in advance for other meals, cost of which will be added to final tariff.

Extra Facilities & Features

Space available for small corporate retreat. Fax, phone, and secretarial service available.

COUNTRY SPUN FARM BED & BREAKFAST

Just off Main Street lies this picturesque sheep farm with its lovely brick colonial Cape Cod built in 1975. Long a destination for knitters, sheep collectors and gardeners, this is home to Pennsylvania's hardest-working sheep. The farm is also a haven for folks seeking delightful accommodations amid southern York County's beautiful hills.

Despite the multitude of local activities and historic sites, the favorite attraction for guests remains the sheep barns. The B & B farm is particularly popular in February and March, when the "maternity wards" are at capacity and there is good skiing at Ski Roundtop and Codorus Park.

For those wishing to combine learning with relaxation, seminars are offered at Spoutwood Farm on sheep-raising and cooking with herbs.

Details

Check in: 2 - 8 p.m. Check out: 10:30 a.m. Deposit/Cancellation Policy: $65 deposit sent or credit card guarantee. All cancellations subject to $20 processing fee, balance refunded if ten days' notice given. Payment: cash, personal check, Master Card, VISA, or Discover. Well-behaved children over 12 welcome. No guest pets. Kennels nearby. No handicap access. Air conditioning in guest rooms only. Off-street parking.

Rates

$65 double occupancy. $20 for third person in room. Best to call several weeks in advance for holiday, convention, and fall foliage weekends.

Bed & Bath

Two guest areas: the Garden Room with its private terrace has a double and a twin bed, and a large bath located in the room; the Overlook Suite also has a double and a twin bed plus expands into a second bedroom which has two twins (or king), and a hall bath separating the two rooms. Designed with the business traveler in mind, rooms have private entrances, televisions, writing tables, and telephones. Comfortably appointed with an eye-appealing blend of country decor accents, antiques, appropriate reproductions.

Breakfast & Extras

In warm weather, served garden-side at the patio, a selection of Martha's original recipes including cheddar creamed eggs on toast, spiced broiled peaches, cranberry orange rolls, juice, coffee or tea. In cooler months, guests can enjoy the view of the countryside from the dining room, where Martha has an admirable crockery collection on display.

Martha & Greg Lau

55 S. Main St., Box 117, Loganville, PA 17342. Phone: (717) 428-1162, 10 a.m. - 9 p.m. Location: York County, 1 mile from I-83 Exit 3.

FIELD & PINE
BED &
BREAKFAST

Mary Ellen & Allan Williams

2155 Ritner Highway, Shippensburg, PA 17257. Phone: (717) 776-7179, best to call before 8 a.m. or after 3 p.m. Location: Cumberland County, off I-81 Newville Exit 11, 3 miles on Route 11. Minutes from Dickenson College and Shippensburg University.

ocated along the main highway that connects Carlisle with points south, this 18th-century limestone farm originally served as an inn and tavern for stagecoaches carrying passengers to the nation's capital. It also functioned as a weigh station for freight wagons. Mature boxwoods line the front walk, sheep graze the fields and stately old pine trees surround the home and its 80 acres of farmland.

Guests will almost always find at least one of the seven working fireplaces crackling away on chilly evenings. In the fall, the hosts roast chestnuts by a fire while guests chat about the day's events.

The Big Spring Limestone Trout Stream, with its phenomenal fishing, is a 1 1/2-mile walk down the road. Arrangements to go horseback riding can be made at a farm 3 miles away.

Details

Check in: 2 p.m. Check out: 11 a.m. Deposit/Cancellation Policy: one night's deposit, refunded, less $10 service charge with five days' cancellation notice. Payment: cash, personal check, MasterCard, or VISA. Children 12 and over welcome. No smoking. Unsuitable for guest pets. Kennels 1 mile away. In residence: a cat, Winter and a golden retriever, Ginger. No handicap access. Air conditioning in guest rooms. Off-street parking.

Rates

$50 - $65 double occupancy. $100 - $120 to reserve two-room suite and sitting area. $20 extra person on roll-away in Blue Room. Two-night minimum for Carlisle car shows. Best to call several months in advance for these and holiday weekends.

Bed & Bath

Three guest rooms. The Lamb Room with two twins and Pasture Room with one double bed, share a large sitting room and bath. This was the original innkeeper's quarters and can be reached by winding staircase from a corner in kitchen. The Blue Room has king-size bed, oriental rug, working fireplace, and private bath in hall. All rooms are stenciled and furnished with selected antiques.

Breakfast & Extras

Served in formal dining room or in front of warm fire in the country kitchen's walk-in fireplace, a full breakfast featuring fresh fruit, orange juice, French toast with peaches and cream, and beverages. Soda and wine offered in afternoons and evenings.

KELLERHAUS

G.F. "Joe" & Mary Jane Keller

1643 Holly Pike, Carlisle, PA 17013. Phone: (717) 249-7481, best to call 6 - 9 p.m. but answering machine other times. Location: Cumberland County, approximately 30 minutes west of Harrisburg, off I-81 Exit 14 E, three miles south on Route 34. About 25 minutes north of Gettysburg. For parents of students attending Dickinson College or the Carlisle War College, the oldest military college in the nation, Kellerhaus is a convenient eight minute drive.

Three decades before the founding of our nation, Carlisle was a frontier post against marauding Indians. During the Revolution it was an arsenal and later headquarters for Washington's troops during the Whiskey Rebellion. In the 1860s Confederate troops invaded. Today, Carlisle is known throughout the world for its car auctions and flea markets, and is something of a mecca to antique collectors and import car aficionados. With the crowds these events attract, the quiet country setting of Kellerhaus is a welcome respite. Situated on 20 rolling acres, this 1797 stone farmhouse with its four working fireplaces was enlarged in the late 1800s. Opening a bed and breakfast was a logical choice for two folks who now have seven grown children and enjoy people.

Guests staying at Kellerhaus are welcome to bring their cross-country skis or hiking shoes and set out through the fields. There is a basketball court for a quick morning workout to shed a few calories after eating Mary Jane's hearty breakfast.

Details

Check in: 6 - 8 p.m. Check out: 1 p.m. Deposit/Cancellation Policy: 50% or one-night's lodging. Seven days' notice for refund. Payment: cash, personal check. Children welcome. No smoking or guest pets. No handicap access. Air conditioning or ceiling fans.

Rates

$50 - $60 double occupancy. $10 for extra person. Two-night minimum for special event weekends.

Bed & Bath

Three guest rooms. Room with king-size bed has private bath. Room with two twins and room with double share clawfoot tub and shower. Furnished with antiques and quilts.

Breakfast & Extras

Served in dining room or on patio, a country breakfast including egg casseroles, waffles, sausage, fresh fruit, breads, muffins, juice and beverages. For parents with children attending college or guests with relatives in area, guests for breakfast are welcome. Cost is $5 per extra person. Upon retiring in the evening, guests will find fruit and snacks placed in their rooms.

LIME LIMOUSIN FARMHOUSE BED & BREAKFAST

In 1778, with the British facing certain defeat, George Line must have decided the future looked bright because he purchased 540 acres of prime Pennsylvania farmland. Nearly 100 years later, Bob's great-grandfather built the present 11-room stone and brick home. It has withstood the test of time with the basic floor plan and look changing little over the years. Modern conveniences were added in the '60s, while the heirloom family furnishings, including the player piano in the parlor were retained. Joan and Bob's grandchildren are the ninth generation of Lines to walk the scenic pastureland.

Besides the Limousin cattle, the Lines also raise asparagus. Visitors in late spring are guaranteed this delectable vegetable for breakfast.

A large lawn with giant sugar maple trees is good for cookouts in the summer. Guests are free to tour the beef farm, hike the woods and cross the stone fences to spot wildlife.

Details

Flexible check in and out. Deposit/Cancellation Policy: one night's stay sent. Refunded, less $10 service charge with five days' notice. Payment: personal check. No credit cards.. Children welcome -- up to two per family. No smoking. Guest pets, horses, cattle kept outside in barn. Air conditioning in two guest rooms. Window fans available. On-farm parking for cars pulling trailers.

Rates

$45 - $55 double occupancy. $55 suite. $10 extra person in room. Sleeping bags permitted. Three-night minimum during auto shows.

Bed & Bath

Two guest rooms, each with king (or two twins) and private bath in room. Private entrance, TV and air conditioning. Suite is two adjoining rooms with bath antique double beds. Furnished with antiques and modern pieces.

Breakfast & Extras

Served in formal dining room, a farm breakfast of French toast or fresh asparagus omelettes, sour cream coffee cake, fresh fruit, and coffee. Guest refrigerator stocked with soft drinks for afternoon refreshments.

Extra Facilities & Features

This is a breeding stock farm. The Limousin cattle raised here for show and sale originate from the Limoges area of France. Inn will board guest cattle and horses. On site is croquet, bocce ball, horseshoes and a private golf driving range.

Joan & Bob Line

2070 Ritner Highway, Carlisle, PA 17013. Phone: (717) 243-1281, best to call evenings. Location: Cumberland County, 1 1/2-miles from I-81 Exit 12 on Route 11 South, or 4 miles from downtown Carlisle.

HERSHEY / DUTCH COUNTRY

Just off the Susquehanna in western Lancaster County, Marietta is one of the few colonial-era-villages that was fortunate enough to have been ignored by 20th-century developers. With its hundreds of restored homes along quiet streets, antique shops and architectural treasures, visitors sense what life might have been like during the times of our forefathers.

Located in the Historic District, the 200-year-old River Inn welcomes guests with its meticulous 18th-century restoration and attention to detail. The six working fireplaces, open stairway, crown molding, and tin lighting add to the colonial atmosphere.

After breakfast, before leaving for a day of sightseeing, guests often enjoy a cup of coffee on the huge enclosed porch, stroll around the formal English gardens, or walk across the street to see the Susquehanna River.

RIVER INN

Details

Check in: 2 - 6 p.m. Check out: 11 a.m. Flexible with advance notice. Deposit/Cancellation Policy: credit card guarantee or 50% balance sent. 25% fee on cancellations with less than seven days' notice. Payment: personal check, MasterCard, VISA. Children over 10 welcome. Smoking on screened porch only. Unsuitable for guest pets. No handicap access. Air conditioning in guest rooms on second floor; central air conditioning on first floor.

Rates

$60-65 double occupancy. $10 extra person in room.

Bed & Bath

Three guest rooms all with private baths, canopied or four-poster queen-size beds. One also has a trundle and twin. One with working fireplace. All have antiques and period reproductions.

Breakfast & Extras

Served on the porch in summer, fireside during winter months, a full country breakfast. Afternoon beverages offered. Candy dishes in guest rooms, chocolate kisses on the pillows, wine for honeymooners.

Extra Facilities & Features

Small meetings up to eight. Catering for lunch or dinner possible. Special corporate rate. Arrangements for dinner with local Amish family can be made.

Joyce & Robert Heiserman

258 W. Front St., Marietta, PA 17547. Phone: (717) 426-2290, answering machine when owners are out. Location: Lancaster County, north on Route 441 to Route 23.

RICE'S WHITE HOUSE

Joan M. Rice

10111 Lincoln Way W., St. Thomas, PA l7252. (717) 369-4224, 9 a.m. - 6 p.m., answering machine other times. Location: Franklin County, 12 miles west of I-81, Exit 6, on Route 30. Close to Chambersburg, Fort London and Bedford. 40 minutes to Gettysburg.

HERSHEY / DUTCH COUNTRY

s major commerce and travel developed between Pittsburgh and Philadelphia, folks living along the Turnpike saw increasing numbers of travelers passing by their doors.

In 1790 a two-story addition was built onto a 20-year-old fieldstone home, establishing a tavern and hotel for weary wayfarers. Today the home is called Rice's White House Inn.

Located in the scenic valley between St. Thomas and Fort London, the site of the earliest Revolutionary battle, this beautiful old home has been completely restored. Furnished with unique and unusual antiques, it is once again open to overnight visitors.

Just as long ago, guests are welcomed into the tavern, where they may play cards or play the piano.

Perhaps the most striking feature of this B & B home is the exquisitely manicured yard. The picturesque split-rail fences, bordered with flowers, and the variety of plantings attest to the owner's horticultural interest. The inside is as beautifully arranged as the outside.

Details

Check in: 3-7 p.m. Check out: ll a.m. Deposit/
Cancellation Policy: personal check or cash. No credit cards. Children over 10 welcome. No guest pets. Smoking in designated areas. In residence: cat, Reilly and outside dog, Bucky. No handicap access. Central air conditioning.

Rates

$65 double occupancy. $15 extra person in room.

Bed & Bath

Three guest rooms. Blue Room with antique canopy shares bath with Pink Room's two antique twin beds. These rooms can be closed off by a hall door and booked as a suite. The Green Room with private bath, has two antique brass and iron double beds, sleeps four. All have antiques, quilts, fresh flowers, bath toiletries and candy.

Breakfast & Extras

Served in formal dining room, a hot breakfast that may include French toast, sausage, fresh fruit and beverages. Afternoon tea, coffee and
snacks in parlor. Evening wine.

Extra Facilities & Features

Meeting room for six to eight persons. Catering for lunch and dinner possible. Hiking and cross-country skiing on mountain area behind house. Bass fishing in stocked pond. Nearby, horses can be boarded and fox hunting arranged.

THE
ADAMSTOWN
INN

I f there is a place antique lovers consider their heaven, it may be Adamstown. Home to 2500 dealers, this charming town with its turn-of-the century atmosphere has often been referred to as the Antique Capital of America. After a day of searching for the perfect 19th-century piece, guests will want to visit the Reading outlets. Only 10 miles away, Reading is home to one of the first true outlet complexes in America. The variety and quantity of shops here would keep even the most diehard shopper occupied for days.

Whatever the reason for a trip to this part of Pennsylvania, visitors have found the Bermans' early 1800s Victorian bed and breakfast an ideal place to relax after a busy day. The expansive Victorian sitting room is a perfect place for guests to gather, read a book or participate in one of the parlor games. Wanda remembers one evening they played Pictionary with a couple while a college professor sat on the floor by the fireplace grading papers. Guests are also welcome to try playing the 1850 pump organ.

When the Bermans purchased their inn, they were first drawn to the distinguished-looking building with its leaded glass doors, stained glass windows and wrap-around porch. The chestnut woodwork and expansive rooms inside charmed them into deciding this was the place for which they had been searching.

Details

Check in: 3 - 6 p.m. Check out: 10 a.m. Deposit/Cancellation Policy: one night's lodging received within ten days of reservation. Refunds sent, less a $15 processing fee if cancelled ten days prior to stay. Payment: cash, personal check, Master Card, or VISA. Children 12 and over welcome. Smoking in designated areas only. Unsuitable for guest pets. Kennels nearby. In residence: Magic, a Brittany spaniel. No handicap access. Guest rooms are air conditioned. Off-street parking.

Rates

$55 - $95 double occupancy. $85 - $95 for suite. $15 for extra person in room. Two-night minimum stay on holidays, weekends, and Antique Extravaganza. Best to call two months in advance for those weekends.

Bed & Bath

Four guest rooms; all with private bath in room, two with two-person jacuzzis. Master bedroom has king-size bed plus one of the two-person jacuzzis. Other rooms have queen or double beds. All furnished with family heirlooms, quilts, lace curtains and a variety of special Victorian touches.

Breakfast & Extras

Wake up to a polite knock at your door and a tray of freshly brewed coffee or tea. Later join other guests in the formal dining room for a delicious breakfast of fresh fruit salad, sausage balls, apple cake, muffins, cereal and beverages. Afternoon tea is offered in the parlor. Guests will find fresh fruit bowls in rooms for late-night snacking.

Extra Facilities & Features

Conference space for up to 12 is available. Catering for lunch and dinner can be arranged. Inquire about special corporate rates for companies who use the inn regularly. Wanda can make arrangements for dinner with local Amish family if advance notice is given.

Tom & Wanda Berman

62 W. Main St., Adamstown, PA 19501. Phone: (215) 484-0800 or (800) 594-4808, anytime. Location: Lancaster County, off PA 76, Exit 21, 3 miles north off Route 272.

APPLE BIN INN

ver 100 years ago this home established its roots in the mainstream of Lancaster County, serving as a general store for village folks who would sip soda and eat ice cream while waiting for the trolley.

Built in 1865, this two-story brick and frame house with many mature shade trees guarding the well-kept lawn, is now the home of the Apple Bin Inn. Still offering travelers a place to relax in comfort before continuing on their journeys, the inn features a charming colonial-style atmosphere. With Debbie's special quilting and needlework talents, plus Barry's wood-working skills, there are distinctive touches throughout.

The apple motif is ever-present. Apples appear everywhere, including on Barry's apple checker boards.

Debbie assembles delicious picnic baskets, as well as made-to-order baskets containing flowers, toiletries, or other specialty items.

Nearby is a variety of historic attractions, including "Wheatland," the home of Pennsylvania's only U.S. President, J. Buchanan, and the oldest home in Lancaster County, the Hans Herr House. There are also outlet malls, craft shops, quilt shops, and the world-famous Farmers' Market, which offers home-grown produce and select baked goods of the Amish and Mennonites.

Details

Check in: 3 p.m. (Sundays 6 p.m.). Check out: 11 a.m. (Sundays 10:30 a.m.). Deposit/Cancellation Policy: one night's deposit or credit card guarantee. Refunded, less 20%, with 48 hours' notice. Payment: cash, personal check, MasterCard, VISA, or American Express. Children over 7 welcome. No smoking inside. Unsuitable for guest pets. Kennels nearby. In residence: school-age daughter, Lauren. Cabin Room opens to patio and has ramp for wheelchair access, but wheelchair cannot access private bathroom. Air conditioning in guest rooms plus ceiling fans. Off-street parking.

Rates

$50 - $70 double occupancy. $65-$85 suite. $15 extra person in room. Two-night minimum stay on holiday weekends.

Bed & Bath

Five guest rooms. Two with private baths in room, plus two-room suite and a third room share hall bath. One room has a balcony. Cabin Room with lots of wood and open-beamed ceiling opens on to the patio. Rooms all furnished with country and colonial bed reproductions (pencil-post, master bed, and acorn-post), stuffed winged chairs, wicker accents, quilts, colonial love seats, fresh flowers, toiletries and cable television.

Breakfast & Extras

Served in dining room or on one of the shaded patios, a hot breakfast featuring a main dish of German apple pancakes, French toast with pecan sauce, or an egg dish casserole. Accompaniments include fruit, breads, muffins, juice and beverages. Afternoon tea and baked goods offered in dining room or patio. Debbie, for an additional charge, will pack a delicious picnic basket lunch and direct guests to a suitable site.

Extra Facilities & Features

Because the Hersheys are cyclists themselves, they have made space available for bike and equipment storage for cyclists touring area. Cycling maps of the area and information upon request. Also special quilting packages and a Thanksgiving weekend package. Inquire about rates and availability. Debbie will arrange evening dinner with local Amish family with advance notice. Debbie is fluent in sign language.

Barry & Debbie Hershey

2835 Willow Street Pike, Willow Street, PA 17584. Phone: (717) 464-5881, call anytime; if not in, answering machine available. Location: Lancaster County, follow Route 272 N, 3 1/2 miles south of Willow Street.

B & B
OF
LANCASTER
COUNTY
R S O

A prosperous Lancaster County ironmaster chose this scenic property in 1848 to build a grand Victorian home overlooking the Conestoga River. This 2 1/2-story, five-bay brick home with its imposing portico entry supported by Tuscan columns, stands witness to the wealth of the original owner.

The current hosts have taken great care to restore the interior to its impressive beginnings.

But perhaps what visitors remember most are the magnificent gardens, manicured lawn, array of wildflowers and hardwood trees that create a true "Garden of Eden." No doubt the wildlife, too, appreciates the care their hosts have taken with their outdoor home. Marilyn claims the rabbits certainly seem to enjoy their share, nibbling at the plants before the buds have opened. Fortunately, Bill plants enough for everyone – rabbits included!

If guests can pull themselves away from all the natural beauty surrounding them, they are only ten minutes from the city of Lancaster. They can also comb the countryside on rental bikes, or follow the Lancaster County covered bridge tour, which goes by Garden of Eden. Hosts are available for a private guided tour through Amish country.

Details

Check in: 4 p.m. Check out: 1 p.m. Deposit/Cancellation Policy: one night deposit upon reservation. Deposit less a $20 service fee returned with one week's cancellation notice. Payment: cash, traveler's check, MasterCard, or VISA. No children, smoking, or guest pets. No handicap access. Air conditioning in guest rooms. Off-street parking.

Rates

$65 - $110 double occupancy. $85 - $110 guest house. Additional person in guest house $15. Best to call three months in advance for holiday weekends. Two-night minimum stay for these weekends.

Bed & Bath

Three guest rooms in the main house plus adjoining "Summer Kitchen" with full kitchen, dining area, bed and bath available for longer term rental. Of the guest rooms, the master suite with private bath has queen-size canopy bed. The Quilt Room with double bed and the Blue Room with two twins share hall bath. Antique furnishings in all rooms; beds have handmade woven coverlets; pieces from hosts' art, fabric, and period clothing collections accent rooms as well as floral arrangements expertly designed by hostess.

Breakfast & Extras

Served in formal dining room or screen porch in full view of gardens, a breakfast of museli, muffins, juice, fresh fruit and beverages. Sunday mornings feature Bill's baked eggs. Marilyn's fresh mint tea is offered during warm summer months. Guests will find a tray of fresh fruit, cheese and crackers in rooms for late evening snacks.

Extra Facilities & Features

The terraced grounds, gardens and woods that surround the home include at least 50 varieties of natural wildflowers, developing beds of perennials, woodsy trails and scores of songbirds. Marilyn, a professional craftswoman and designer, teaches a variety of classes, including those on beginning and advanced floral design and decorating with herbs. Her home decor reflects her special talent.

Garden of Eden

For reservations contact: Bed & Breakfast of Lancaster County, Box 19, Mountville, PA 17554. Coordinator: Pat Reno. Phone: (717) 285-7200, mornings best, leave message other times. Bed & Breakfast of Lancaster is a reservation service that represents prescreened and inspected properties throughout south central Pennsylvania, including Adams, Bucks, Dauphin and Lancaster counties.

BECHTEL MANSION INN

Built by a prominent local banker in 1897, the Bechtel Mansion is one of 15 key properties listed on the National Register of Historic Places and located in the Historic District of this pre-Revolutionary Pennsylvania German town.

The Bechtel Mansion's Queen Anne style reminds one of what a novelist's imagination might consider the ideal setting for a 19th-century Gothic romance. The turret rooms and balconies, intricately etched glass in doors and bay windows, unusual crystal and brass chandeliers, and period furnishings all lend themselves to a 19th-century plot with damsels in distress and heroes rushing to their aid. Perhaps it is because of this aura that honeymooners and anniversary couples find the inn so appealing.

Many of the 28 rooms, besides having many heirloom and antique furnishings and brass chandeliers, also feature beautiful built-in cupboards and wardrobes made of cherry, chestnut or oak. The formal parlor, which has the original wallpaper and Brussels carpet, is part of the Downstairs Suite.

Behind the mansion, a Victorian Carriage House has been insulated, electrified, and customized to serve as a charming antique shop and guest quarters. There are sleeping facilities for a limited number of bicyclists and country living enthusiasts at $44 double occupancy, which includes a continental breakfast. A full bath in the lower level of the mansion serves Carriage House guests.

Details

Check in: 1 - 6 p.m. Check out: 11 a.m. Deposit/Cancellation Policy: reservations accepted on a guaranteed basis via personal check or credit card. Seventy-two hour cancellation notice required to avoid charges. Payment: cash, personal check, MasterCard, VISA, American Express, Discover. Children of all ages welcome. Smoking permitted on porches and balconies only. No guest pets, but kennels approximately 6 miles away. Air conditioning in guest rooms, dining room, and breakfast rooms. No handicap access.

Rates

$70 - $100 double occupancy. $125 - $135 suites. Rollaways $20. 5% service charge added to bill. Best to call six to eight weeks in advance for holiday and special event weekends. Two-night minimum stay holidays and October weekends.

Bed & Bath

Seven guestrooms and two suites; six with bath in room, one with bath in hall, two share a bath; most with stall showers and no tub. Seven rooms have one double bed, one has a queen bed, one has two twins. The Downstairs Suite has one and a half baths. The Balcony Suite has the original 1897 claw-foot tub. The Turret Room, Parents Room, and Balcony Suite each have a private balcony.
Furnished with antiques. Many of the brass and crystal chandeliers are original to mansion.

Breakfast & Extras

Served in the formal dining room featuring an extensive collection of heirloom china and an unusual walnut table, tall gilded pier mirror, and etched glass windows, breakfast featuring fruit ambrosia, coffee cake, ham or corn muffins, cheese biscuits, pear and apple butters, schmierkase cheese and coffee or tea. Afternoon beverages and evening wine offered.

Extra Facilities & Features

Conference space available for up to ten. Third floor living room also adaptable for meeting use. Catering for lunch or dinner can be arranged. Special romantic packages for two for anniversary and honeymoon couples. Gift shop specializes in Amish dolls, solid oak furniture and locally-made crafts.

Ruth Spangler, Innkeeper
Charles & Mariam Bechtel, Owners

400 W. King St., East Berlin, PA 17316. Phone: (717) 259-7760, Mon., Tues., Fri., 9 a.m. - 6 p.m. and evenings 7 -9 p.m., answering machine other times. Location: Adams County, 18 miles east of Gettysburg, use Route 234. Exit off Route 15, proceed 8 miles to East Berlin.

BRAFFERTON INN

In 1786, James Gettys bought 116 acres of prime Pennsylvania farm land from his father, who had gone bankrupt supporting the Revolution. James drew up a new town plan and on November 30, 1787, sold his first lot. Soon a rubble construction fieldstone house was erected and the village of Gettysburg was born. Little did James know that barely 75 years later, his quiet little town would become the site of one of our nation's most significant historical events. Now that same stone structure houses the Brafferton Inn, sharing its varied history with its guests.

During the Civil War, as Union troops were pushed through the center of town, shots rang out and shattered the glass in an upstairs window. The bullet lodged in the fireplace mantle where it remains for guests to see to this day. As the battle raged, the Catholic Church became a hospital, and parish services were moved to the Codori House (later to become the Brafferton). Troops flanked the stairs as worshippers walked up to their temporary sanctuary. The troops are gone now but many visitors to the Brafferton have mentioned feeling a strange chill as they ascend those stairs.

Today guests will appreciate a restoration that attests to the fact that the Brafferton was Jim's eighth project. Throughout the inn, guests will notice several recurring accents: multitude of old *Life* magazines and Civil War books, bits of a rather extensive hat collection, humorous British masks in every bedroom and stencils reproduced from the 1700s.

Details

Check in: 2 p.m. Check out: 11 a.m. Deposit/Cancellation Policy: credit card guarantee or 50% of stay sent in advance. Refunded if seven days' notice given. Payment: cash, personal check, MasterCard or VISA. Children over 7 welcome. Smoking in designated areas only. Unsuitable for guest pets, but kennels nearby. In residence: poodle, Quincy, and perhaps a visit from one of their five adult children depending upon the time of year. Handicap access on first floor guest rooms. Air conditioning in guest rooms. Off-street parking.

Rates

$70 - $110 double occupancy. $10 additional person in room. Best to call four months in advance for holiday and Gettysburg College weekends. Two-night minimum stay during these times.

Bed & Bath

Eleven guest rooms. Seven with private baths in room, four rooms share two additional bathrooms. All with antique double beds. Four rooms also have a single bed. The quilts, period furnishing, stenciling on whitewash walls, unique accent pieces, oil paintings, samplers, and prints create a feeling of traveling back in time. The use of antique double-size beds rather than modern day queen or king was intentional to maintain the 1786 period of the house.

Breakfast & Extras

Served in the dining room with its wonderful primitive mural depicting 18 of Gettysburg's historic buildings, an ample breakfast featuring peaches and cream, French toast, strawberry blintzes, Canadian bacon, fruit, juice, and beverages.

Extra Facilities & Features

Conference space available for small business meetings. Phones in each room. Catering can be arranged for lunch or dinner. Special corporate rate. Lovely decked garden in back planted with typical 18th- and 19th-century herbs and flowers. Sunny glass-covered atrium nestled between the old stone house and the brick addition. Parlor's player piano is often a gathering place for guests enjoying an evening sing-along. Ask about special ongoing weekend packages.

Mimi & Jim Agard

44 York St., Gettysburg, PA 17325. Phone: (717) 337-3423, anytime. Location: Adams County, use Route 30 Exit off Route 15, travel west 1 mile to York Street, in the heart of historic Gettysburg.

CHURCHTOWN INN

Built in 1735, this three-story stone colonial home was owned by Edward Davies, member of the 25th Congress and a state legislator. The Georgian Federal section he added in 1804 distinguishes the Churchtown as a home for gentry.

Now this impeccably restored inn is the most prominent landmark in the Pennsylvania Dutch hamlet of Churchtown. Situated on a ridge between picture-postcard valleys and Amish farmland, it is only minutes from all of the attractions of Lancaster County.

Furnished with antiques, collectibles, including a music box collection, personal treasures, fresh flowers, and a warm spirit, Churchtown is so relaxed and confortable that many guests become repeat visitors.

It's fun, too! The innkeepers offer an array of weekend packages that are unrivaled. There is barely a weekend from November through May that is without a special theme or event. Their complete annual program offering weekends that feature everything from a Victorian Ball to Murder Mysteries is available upon request.

With Jim's and Stuart's varied musical backgrounds, which include travel with worldwide concert tours, the Churchtown Inn is a haven for artists. As a result, impromptu evening concerts or sing-alongs at the baby grand are common evening occurrences.

Before departing this quiet little town, guests often wander across the street to peer in at the Historic Bangor Episcopal Church established in 1753 or stroll through the cemetery reading the worn headstones, some more than two centuries old.

Details

Check in: 2 p.m. Check out: 11 a.m.
Deposit/Cancellation Policy: one-night's
stay with credit card guarantee.
Refunded if eight days' notice given.
Payment: cash or personal check
preferred. MasterCard or VISA
accepted. Children 12 and over
welcome. Smoking permitted in
designated areas, but no cigars or pipes.
Unsuitable for guest pets. Carriage
House is ground level handicap
accessible, but no handrails. Air
conditioning in all rooms. Off-street
parking.

Rates

$75 - $95 double occupancy rooms with
private bath. $49 - $59 double
occupancy rooms with shared bath.
$125 for Carriage House. $20 for extra
person in room. Two-night minimum
stay on weekends, three-night minimum
stay on holiday weekends. Best to call
one month or more in advance for these
times.

Bed & Bath

Eight romantic guest rooms; six with
private bath, two share a bath, all located
on second and third floors. A separate
Carriage House. All have queen or
single beds, handmade quilts, lace
linens, and are filled with antiques and
collectibles from all over Europe. The
Carriage House offers a very private
accommodation for special occasions.
It has private entrance, king-size bed,
private bath, Victorian furnishings,
Oriental rug and crystal chandelier.

Breakfast & Extras

Served in either the formal dining room
or on the glass-enclosed Breakfast Room
that overlooks the well-tended herb and
flower gardens and Welsh mountains;
using crystal stemware and fine china,
an unbelievable multiple-course
breakfast. Upon being seated, there is a
selection of cereals, fresh fruit, juices and
beverages (the tea cozies come from
Europe). The hot entree may include
Grand Marnier French toast, high-rise
apple pancakes, delectable souffles, or
an English oatmeal custard. To end,
there is a fruit parfait and freshly-baked
coffee cake. Evenings, guests are invited
to sit and chat in the parlor over
beverages and snacks.

Extra Facilites & Features

Space available for conferences or
receptions, up to 25 people. Two rooms
available; the Carriage House can be
converted as well. For weekend guests
with advance notice, Stuart can make
arrangements for Saturday evening
dinner with a local Amish family. Cost
is $12 per person. On three-day
summer holiday weekends, guests can
choose to enjoy an on-site barbecue and
musical entertainment. Cost is $10 per
person. Candlelit evening dinners can
also be arranged. Cost varies.
Innkeepers will map out local tours
upon request.

Hermine & Stuart Smith, Jim Kent

*Mailing address: 2100 Main St., Narvon,
PA 17555. Phone: (215) 445-7794, 10
a.m. - 10 p.m., answering machine other
times. Location: Lancaster County, off PA
Turnpike Exit 22, continue 5 miles on
Route 23 west to Churchtown.*

CLEARVIEW
FARM
BED &
BREAKFAST

In 1814 George and Catherine Lawyer laid the cornerstone of their 11-room limestone farmhouse. In 1959 Glen and Mildred Wissler bought the farmhouse and its surrounding 200 acres.

Cleaning, fixing and modernizing, the Wisslers made it their dream home. Three decades later they did it all again. True to the times, their first "restoration" paid more attention to modernization than preservation. Gone is an old wood mantel and chair railings, to make way for larger, more modern rooms. Despite their first modernization, the integrity of the house survived and their recent restoration has created a charming home where guests instantly feel welcome.

Once-carpeted floors gave way to random-width boards measuring up to 19 inches wide. Ceiling beams and stone walls were exposed, while a corner fireplace that escaped the earlier tearing-out was uncovered during the latest, "if we had only known then what we know now" stage.

The idea of opening a bed and breakfast struck them during one of their many auction-hunting journeys that have led them from Massachusetts to Virginia in search of the perfect piece. Now their new "old" home is completely furnished with carefully-chosen and tastefully- displayed antiques and collectibles.

Today, as guests pull up to the farm, chances are good they'll be greeted by at least one friendly duck and a peacock or two. Outside, the well-tended gardens, spacious manicured lawn and swans gliding along the pond create a picture-postcard setting that prompts many first-time guests to get out the camera even before they knock at the Wisslers' door.

Details

Check in: 5 - 9 p.m. Check out: 10 a.m. Deposit/Cancellation Policy: one night's stay sent one month in advance. Refunds with 48-hour notice or if room can be re-rented. Payment: cash, personal check, MasterCard, or VISA. Unsuitable for children or guest pets. Smoking permitted on outside porches. No handicap access. Central air conditioning. Off-street parking.

Rates

$55 - $69 double occupancy. Best to call two months in advance for special weekends and holidays. Two-night minimum stay these times.

Bed & Bath

Five guest rooms. Three with private bath in room, two rooms share hall bath. The Royal Room has ornately carved walnut Victorian bed and etagere. The private bath has clawfoot tub and shower. The Garden Room has antique queen-size iron and brass bed while the Princess Room has lace-embellished queen-size canopy bed and Victorian marble-top dresser. The Lincoln Room with its country flair and queen-size pencil-post bed and the Washington Room with queen-size canopy display the third floor's hand-pegged rafters, exposed stone walls and original wide board flooring. All rooms have a sitting area for reading and relaxing. Gilt framed prints, Oriental rugs, potted ferns and fresh flowers accent the rooms.

Breakfast & Extras

Served in a Victorian dining room using beautiful crystal and china table settings, or weather permitting, in screened-in porch. A country breakfast includes fresh fruit, muffins, ham and cheese souffle with home fries, and beverages. Served Monday through Sunday.

Glen & Mildred Wissler

355 Clearview Road, Ephrata, PA 17522. Phone: (717) 733-6333. Location: Lancaster County, use PA Turnpike Exit 21, north on Route 272, then west on Route 322. Close to Ephrata Cloister and Landis Valley Museum.

COLUMBIAN

In the 1790s, the bustling river town of Columbia found itself on the short list of contenders for the site of the nation's capital. Perhaps fortunately for this charming town, our founding fathers decided the Potomac rather than the Susquehanna provided the better location.

Coming here is like visiting a town suspended in time. The local drugstore boasts a lunch counter where you can still get a vanilla coke or a malted. A brief stroll of the streets reveals countless restored homes, one of which had an appointment with the city's wrecking ball until the Straitiffs rescued it from destruction. Built in 1898, this historically registered Colonial Revival brick home housed three apartments and a video store until the Straitiffs spent months restoring it to its original splendor. Now, upon entering, instead of seeing tenants' mailboxes and video tapes, guests are greeted by an unusual tiered staircase with an enormous four-section stained-glass window.

The most popular rooms are the sitting room and the dining room, both with unusual corner fireplaces offering warm comfort on chilly days.

Located on the western edge of Lancaster County, Columbia is only a short distance from the Amish farms, but visitors often find Columbia itself so intriguing they never get any farther. Here, the headquarters and museum of The National Association of Clock and Watch Collectors is located, plus the Susquehanna Glass Factory, Wrights Ferry Museum, Columbia Farmers Market and numerous antique shops.

Details

Check in: 3 p.m. Check out: 12 noon. Deposit/Cancellation Policy: $20 per room reserved or credit card guarantee. Refunded with 24 hours notice. Payment: cash, personal check, MasterCard, VISA, American Express, or Discover. Children over 12 welcome. No smoking inside. Unsuitable for guest pets. Kennels nearby. In residence: two teenage sons, Joe and John, during summer; friendly dog Bear year-round. Air conditioning in guest rooms and common areas. No handicap access. Off-street parking.

Rates

$55 - $70 double occupancy. Bucher Suite $70. $10 extra person in room. Sleeping bags permitted, but extra charge applies. Special corporate rate. Best to call several weeks in advance for peak weekends and holidays.

Bed & Bath

Four rooms and one suite, all named after former owners, all with private baths. The Ladies' Parlor with working fireplace, Yost Room, and Bishop Room all have one queen. The Moore Room has one queen and one twin, and the Bucher Suite with private balcony and sitting room, has one queen, queen sleeper, and twin in adjoining room. Beds, all with antique headboards and footboards, are on custom designed platforms. Baths have all been creatively built out of the rooms' former trunk closets or wardrobe areas and are very nicely done. Furnishings which reflect Linda and John's penchant for collectibles and talent for restoring antiques include a comfortable mixture of auction finds, garage sale bargains, 19th century antiques, and pieces from Linda's plate, doll, and bottle collections. Toiletries, fresh flowers and fruit are provided in each room.

Breakfast & Extras

Served fireside in formal dining room, a filling breakfast that includes grapefruit half, assorted cereals, cherry cobbler, peaches and cream French toast, quiche Lorraine, fresh fruit salad, sausage or ham, juice and beverages. Upon special request, breakfast can be served in guest rooms. The unusual wrap-around sunporches are a popular place to sip ice tea and lemonade, while the sitting room is where guests gather evenings for a cup of hot tea and to make dinner plans. With advance notice, Linda can arrange dinner with an Amish family.

Linda & John Straitiff

360 Chestnut St., Columbia, PA 17512. Phone: (717) 684-5869 or (800) 422-5869, anytime; answering machine when not available. Location: Lancaster County, 8 miles west of the city of Lancaster near Route 30.

GOOSE CHASE
BED &
BREAKFAST

*D*ne wonders what was on John Leese's mind as he guided his mount down the narrow dirt road. Leaving behind his log cabin and family to fight in the Revolutionary War, he undoubtedly had concerns about what the future would bring his family and his state.

The property was originally part of a 300-acre land grant from William Penn. The first cabin was built in 1759, and limestone sections were added over the years.

Now guests travel down the same country lane that John Leese followed to a peaceful, scenic farm that is home to Goose Chase Inn. Completely restored, down to the original floorboards, ceiling beams, and deep-silled windows, the 18th-century home even reflects a careful selection of paint colors.

Guests find the atmosphere inviting and fun. In fact, one guest wrote, "anyone who can grow Shitaaki mushrooms, write unsolvable murders, and cook to boot is definitely worth meeting---how terrific that your talents turn into such fun for the rest of us!"

In their "spare" time after caring for their guests, the innkeepers also tend to geese, sheep, and two mischievous goats. The constant profusion of bulbs, flowering trees, fragrant herb gardens, and blooming perennials creates a peaceful retreat from city life.

Nature trails, abundant wildlife and a charming pond complete the picture of a quiet, restful setting. The isolated feeling of the inn causes folks to forget they are only minutes away from all of south central Pennsylvania's countless attractions, including the Gettysburg Battlefield.

Details

Check in: 4 p.m. Check out: 12 noon. Deposit/Cancellation Policy: $25 per night per room deposit, completely refunded if cancelled within ten days of reservations. Payment: cash, personal check, MasterCard, or VISA. Children over 10 welcome. No smoking. No handicap access. Unsuitable for guest pets. Kennels nearby. Central air conditioning. Off-street parking.

Rates

$69 - $89 double occupancy. $10 for additional person in room. Children's sleeping bags permitted (extra charge applies).

Bed & Bath

Five guest rooms. Three with private bath in room, two share bath in hall. Jefferson Room has antique rope bed and is on first floor. Franklin Room has king-size bed; Madison Room, two twins; Abigail Adams Room, canopied queen bed and working fireplace; and Martha Washington Room, four-poster queen bed and working fireplace. All rooms furnished with 18th-century antique or period reproductions, stenciling on walls, Oriental rugs, and Williamsburg decor. Fresh flowers, toiletries, potpourri, and terry robes are also found in rooms.

Breakfast & Extras

Served in colonial dining room by Marsha in period costume, a delicious breakfast of fresh fruit compote with yogurt dressing, bran muffins, crepe a'la Lucidi, ham, sausage or bacon, the ever-present blueberries and beverages. Summer afternoon guests relax on patio with fresh mint tea or lemonade. Winter brings mulled cider served by a crackling fireplace. Chocolates found on pillows at bedtime.

Extra Facilities & Features

Appropriate for small corporate retreats for up to seven participants. Catering for lunch and dinner can be arranged. Special corporate rate. In-ground pool, cross-country skiing and hiking trails. Guests can pick own blueberries in season. Special anniversary package that includes champagne with dinner plus breakfast in bed. Cooking classes and Murder Mystery Weekends offered year around. Call about schedules for these and other weekend packages.

Marsha & Rich Lucidi

200 Blueberry Road, Gardners, PA 17324. Phone: (717) 528-8877, best to call evenings; answering machine other times. Location: Adams County, 3 miles from Route 234 Exit 15 N, about 15 minutes from Gettysburg.

GREYSTONE MANOR BED & BREAKFAST

ore than a dozen old hotel and tavern signs have lent their names to Pennsylvania villages and hamlets. One example is the charming village of Bird-In-Hand, located in the heart of Lancaster County's Amish country.

Down the road from the old Bird-In-Hand hotel visitors will find Greystone Manor Bed and Breakfast. This French Victorian mansion, the town's finest existing late Victorian residence, was constructed in 1883 from a farmhouse built in the mid-1800s. Behind the mansion is the Carriage House, now used for guests.

With all of Lancaster County's tourist attractions nearby, guests often don't have time to enjoy the two acres of gardens and grounds that have been painstakingly developed. However, anyone who takes a few moments for a morning cup of coffee on the patio, will be entertained watching the resident squirrel steal corn off the feeder.

The Victorian lobby, with its beveled glass doors, plaster cast walls, and ceiling sculptures, offers guests a quiet place to relax.

Details

Check in: 2 - 8 p.m. Check out: 11 a.m. Deposit/Cancellation Policy: first night's lodging forwarded via check or money order, refunded with 48 hours notice, or if room is rebooked. Payment: cash, personal check, MasterCard, or VISA. Children welcome. Smoking permitted in Carriage House. Unsuitable for guest pets. No handicap access. Central air conditioning. Off-street parking.

Rates

Rooms: in season, $58 - $74; off season, $46 - $60. Suites: in season, $68 - $84; off season, $54 - $68. $10 for third person in room. $6 for each additional person. Best to call one month in advance for reservations during peak season.

Bed & Bath

Seven rooms and six two-room suites for families. All with private bath in room. Five rooms have access to a balcony. Rooms and suites have one or two beds, sizes and combinations vary using king, queen, and double beds. The seven rooms in the mansion have a Victorian motif, six rooms in Carriage House have a country flair. Several feature such items as stained-glass windows, cut crystal doors, original woodword, and antique bath fixtures. The Carriage House is the original barn, converted in 1970 to its present form. All rooms have televisions, air conditioning and modern amenities affording guests comfortable, clean lodging.

Breakfast & Extras

Served in formal dining room, a choice of juice, homebaked muffins and beverages. Wedding and anniversary couples will find homemade chocolate treats in rooms.

Extra Facilites & Features

Conference space available for up to 15. Special corporate rate. On premises is a quilt and craft shop, featuring locally-made quilts at reasonable prices.

Sally Davis

2655 Old Philadelphia Pike, P. O. Box 270, Bird-In-Hand, PA 17505. Phone: (717) 393-4233, 8 a.m. - 8 p.m.; answering machine other times. Location: Lancaster County, on the south side of Route 340, 1 block west of Bird-In-Hand overpass.

GUESTHOUSE & 1777 HOUSE AT DONECKERS

The year was 1777 and at 301 W. Main St. in Ephrata, Jacob Gorgas toiled at molding brass and burnishing wood for some of the 150 Eight Day Gorgas Grandfather clocks he created in his lifetime. Many are highly valued and still in working order.

With the passage of time came new roles for the house. It has served as a tavern for families crossing Penns Woods from Philadelphia to Pittsburgh in Conestoga wagons, as an elegant inn during the early 1900s, and now as the stately 1777 House at Doneckers. With special intent to preserve the integrity of the house, careful restoration has retained original stone masonry, handsome tile flooring, and many authentic details.

Just a few blocks away is the Guesthouse located in the Doneckers Community. Here each of the 19 rooms has an inviting personality with special touches like cozy fireplaces, bubbling jacuzzi baths and luxurious suites.

At the Doneckers Community, visitors delight in shopping at the classic and sophisticated fashion stores. There are four main shops, one for women, a men's shop and Young World with its miniature barn and barnyard where little ones are invited to play while Mom and Dad shop. Doneckers Home Fashions is popular with anyone who longs for the finest accessories life can offer for the bed, bath, dining room and patio.

At the Artworks, visitors will find a showplace for working artists and fine craftspersons, plus year-round exhibitions and antique and crafts shows.

Details

Check in: 3 p.m. Check out: 11 a.m.
Deposit/Cancellation Policy: credit card
guarantee or one night's deposit sent in
advance. Refunded 48 hours prior to
reservation if cancelled. Payment: cash,
personal check, MasterCard, VISA,
American Express, Diners Club, or
Discover. Children welcome.
Unrestricted smoking is permitted. No
guest pets; kennels nearby. Ramp for
handicap access to first-floor rooms.
Central air conditioning. Off-street
parking.

Rates

$59 - $89 double occupancy. $115 with
jacuzzi. Suites are $135 - $175. Crib is $8
per night. Cot is $10 per night. Holiday
weekends: two-night minimum. Best to
call one month in advance.

Bed & Bath

Between the two properties, there are 31
rooms and suites, 29 with private baths,
many with jacuzzis, and beds are
primarily queen-size. Six have working
fireplaces in room. All guest rooms and
suites have been elegantly furnished
with a selection of exquisitely hand-
painted antiques, unusual hand-hooked
rugs, handcut stenciling on walls, folk
art, and a tasteful selection of country
accents. The 19 distinctive rooms at
Guesthouse all follow a particular
theme, depending upon the historically
prominent local person or place for
which the room has been named. The 12
rooms and suites at the 1777 House have
all been named for a religious member of
the Ephrata Cloister.

Breakfast & Extras

Served in a charming stonewalled
breakfast room with a small fireplace
and varying size tables, a buffet
breakfast featuring fresh pastries,
breakfast cheese, fresh fruit, baked
apples, sausage, cereals, juice and
beverages. Weather permitting, there is
also seating on outside patios. Guests
will find a fruit basket in room for a mid-
day snack and chocolates by the bed at
night. Delightful evening dining is
created by a renowned chef who blends
French traditions with the freshest foods
creating cuisine with imagination and
superb taste.

Extra Facilities & Features

Small meeting room available. Fax
available. Phones in each room. Catering
for lunch or dinner can be arranged.
Doneckers Community also comprised
of fine fashion stores, the Artworks, and
full-service gourmet restaurant.

Jan Grobengeiser, Innkeeper
H. William Donecker, Owner

*318-322 N. State St. (Guesthouse), 301 W.
Main St. (1777 House), Ephrata, PA
17522. Phone: (717) 733-8696, best to call 8
a.m. - 8 p.m.; answering machine other
times. Location: Lancaster County, use PA
Turnpike Exit 21, Route 222 South to
Ephrata Exit, 4 1/2 miles to Route 322 into
Ephrata.*

HERR
FARMHOUSE
INN

When this Pennsylvania Plantation house was built in 1738, farmers tilled the rolling hillsides by hand, and the occasional caller arrived on horseback. Little has changed in the scenic farmlands of Lancaster County, except today it is the horses and not the farmers that pull the plows.

Thanks to Barry Herr's meticulous restoration, little too has changed at the limestone farmhouse. Visitors can easily imagine a time long ago when kettles hung in the kitchen's walk-in hearth and bubbled over with the evening meal. Six fireplaces still burn brightly, warming the parlor, dining room, and bedrooms.

Distinctive features, like the fanlights adorning the main entrance, original pine floors and moldings, and even a restored beehive oven, all add to the ambiance of this charming 18th-century inn.

Outside there are a number of intact outbuildings, attesting to the fact that this was a working farm many years ago. With the exception of the only resident livestock, Clyde the cat, it is primarily a non-working farm today.

Located only 9 miles from the city of Lancaster and all its major Amish attractions, Herr Farmhouse offers guests a quiet evening in the library or in the game room, where there's a player piano.

The cozy red flannel nightshirts that are provided along with the thick bed quilts make "snuggling in" on cold winter nights one of the many memories guests later recall about their visit to the Herr Farmhouse Inn.

Details

Check in: 4 p.m. Check out: 10:30 a.m. Deposit/Cancellation Policy: 50% of reservation total with a check or credit card guarantee. One week's notice for cancellation - full refund. Three day notice - refund less $10 handling fee. Less than three days, no refund unless rebooked. Payment: cash, personal check, MasterCard, or VISA. Children over 10 welcome. Smoking permitted in designated areas. Unsuitable for guest pets. In residence: one cat, Clyde. No handicap access. Central air conditioning. Off-street parking. Also owned by innkeeper is the 1850s Alden House in historic Lititz.

Rates

$70 - $80 double occupancy. $95 suite. $10 for extra person in room. Best to call one month in advance for holiday weekends. Two-night minimum these weekends.

Bed & Bath

Three guest rooms and one suite. The Lancaster Room with private bath and fireplace has full-size canopy bed situated at just the right angle for gazing into the crackling fireplace. The Mt. Joy Room with full-size canopy shares a hall bath with the Lititz Room, which has a fireplace and antique rope bed, equipped with box spring and mattress. The Penthouse suite has two rooms, one with two twins and one with double bed, private bath, beautiful view. All rooms are furnished with colonial-era antiques, Amish quilts, and old blanket chests and trunks.

Breakfast & Extras

Served during cooler months in a country kitchen that has a large walk-in fireplace and an extensive collection of antique farm implements and tools hung from the wall; weather permitting, in the bright airy sun room, a breakfast of freshly baked muffins, breads, Wisconsin cheese, fruit, cereal and beverages. Enjoy afternoon tea and snacks in the parlor or on one of the front porch rockers, taking in the bucolic farm scenery.

Barry A. Herr

2256 Huber Drive, Manheim, PA 17545. Phone: (717) 653-9852, best to call after 4 p.m.; answering machine other times. Location: Lancaster County, 9 miles west of Lancaster, just off Route 283.

KING'S COTTAGE

orse-drawn buggies trotting alongside gas-powered vehicles would seem incongruous in any other community. But this is Lancaster County. No other region in Pennsylvania can claim such an unlikely mixture of cultures, nationalities and religious sects. For 250 years, the people of Lancaster have been accepting of new ideas, tolerant of the unusual and careful to nurture a sense of unity amid diversity. Therefore, when a Spanish mission-style mansion began taking shape at the corner of King and Cottage in 1913, it's doubtful so much as an eyebrow was raised. Unique in Lancaster, it featured the white stucco walls, red clay tile roof and irregularly shaped windows common to an architectural style usually found in the southwest.

Three-quarters of a century later, the mansion was in desparate need of repair when Karen and Jim Owens began to reclaim its original grandeur. Since the mansion opened in 1987, their efforts have been acknowledged by various historical societies, and rewarded with a listing on the National Register.

Inside the Owens have captured the essence of the eclectic styles prevelant in 1913. But the real emphasis is on personal service. Among the guests who have enjoyed the Owens' hospitality is Pennsylvania Governor Robert Casey. Besides arranging Amish dinners for guests, Karen will set up personalized Mennonite guided tours. Their restaurant comment book is rife with notations from guests' experiences at local eateries. On Tuesdays and Fridays guests will be directed to one of several farmers' markets where everything from freshly ground horseradish to scrapple to shoofly pie can be purchased.

Details

Check in: 4 - 7 p.m. Check out: 11 a.m. Deposit/Cancellation Policy: 50% of total bill due within seven days of securing reservation. Refunded, less $15 processing fee, with seven days' notice prior to date. Less than seven days' notice, deposit is forfeited unless room is rebooked. Payment: cash or personal check preferred, but MasterCard, or VISA accepted. Children 12 and over welcome. Smoking not permitted inside. Unsuitable for guest pets. No handicap access. Central air conditioning. Off-street parking.

Rates

$75 - $115 double occupancy. King and Queen Suite $190. $25 for additional person in room. Best to call two months in advance for major weekends and holidays. Two-night minimum stay on all weekends, and three-night minimum on some holidays.

Bed & Bath

Seven guest rooms, all named for royalty. Three with private bath in room and four with private bath in hall, with fluffy bathrobes provided. Baths feature large tubs for a leisurely soak; one of the original baths has a separate shower and extra large tub. Baths may have antique pedestal sinks, marble antique washstands, or stained glass windows. All have queen- or king-size beds and, befitting their names, are regally furnished with an unmatched selection of vintage antiques, appropriate reproductions, and colorful Oriental and woven wool rugs. Rooms and bath also contain signature toiletries, artfully done silk flower arrangements and exquisite window treatments. The King and Queen Rooms have an adjoining pocket door allowing them to be used as a two-room suite, while the Princess Room features the only private balcony and overlooks the lily pond.

Breakfast & Extras

Served in the formal dining room at an elegantly appointed table, a menu that reflects the time Karen spends in searching for unusual recipes. Some of the guests' favorites include a cold peach soup with a dollop of creme fraiche, thick apple pancake platter, a plum torte, fresh fruit compote accompanied with locally-made country sausage, freshly squeezed orange juice and a selection of hot beverages. Afternoons feature hot cider or iced tea plus a homebaked snack such as coconut, oatmeal, pecan pie. Evenings, guests find turned-down bed with mints on their pillows and enjoy cordials in the library before retiring.

Extra Facilities & Features

Corporate meeting space for small conferences up to 12 participants. Catering for lunch and dinner can be arranged. Special corporate rates. Dinners with an Amish family can be arranged.

Karen & Jim Owens

1049 E. King St., Lancaster, PA 17602. Phone: (717) 397-1017 or (800) 747-8717, best to call 10 a.m. - 7 p.m., answering machine other times. Location: Lancaster County, five minutes from both downtown Lancaster and Amish country attractions, at the corner of King Street (Route 462) and Cottage Avenue.

LIMESTONE INN

Two hundred years ago, as the Chief Burgess of Strasburg looked out his windows, horses and buggies passed close by his front door. Today, the horses and buggies still travel past this elegant limestone residence, built in 1786. Strasburg's first post office once stood on this site. From 1839 to 1860 up to 50 boys attended the famous Strasburg Academy, which was erected behind the home.

Architecturally as well as historically, this building ranks among Lancaster County's most important. Although based on a formal, symmetrical five-bay Georgian house plan with a central hallway, the building has some Germanic overtones, making it a link between early colonial and purely formal Georgian architecture.

The home's former keeping room now serves as a gathering place for guests, who may choose a book from the extensive library, relax by the fireplace, or play a game of cards with other visitors. There is even a player piano for folks who appreciate more lively entertainment!

In the backyard there is a formal courtyard with a small sitting area where guests are often seen sorting through their maps and brochures, planning their activities. If advice is needed, Jan is well-versed in colonial history and is happy to share her knowledge of the area's history with her guests. With her use of 18th-century dress at breakfast, the tone is set for a busy day of sightseeing, antique hunting, or just driving through the picturesque countryside.

Details

Check in: 4 - 7 p.m. Check out: 11 a.m. Deposit/Cancellation Policy: 50% deposit sent, refunded less $10 service fee, if cancelled at least seven days prior to reservation. Payment: cash, personal check, or American Express. Children 12 and over welcome. Cigarette smoking in designated areas; pipes and cigars outside. Unsuitable for guest pets. In residence: two miniature schnauzers, Max and Betsy. No handicap access. Central air conditioning. Off-street parking.

Rates

$65 - $80 double occupancy. A 10% discount on a stay of four or more nights during Sundays through Thursdays, except holidays, from November 15 - May 15. $20 for extra person in room. Best to call four to six weeks in advance for major weekends. Two-night minimum stay on holiday weekends.

Bed & Bath

Six rooms provide three shared or private hall baths. On second floor, one room has queen, other has two twins. These rooms are large enough for a rollaway. A long narrow hall leads to the four quaint rooms on the third floor, all with double beds, that were once part of the dormitory occupied by the academy students. Today, these rooms still bear the initials of the students on the wood moldings and doors. These rooms contain standard double beds. Obvious effort has been made, while keeping the guests' comfort in mind, to retain the flavor of an 18th-century residence throughout the inn. The guest rooms, furnishings and accessories include primitive antiques, Amish quilts, handknit 18th-century reproduction bed throws, wall hangings and even the necessary chamber pot in each room!

Breakfast & Extras

Served promptly at 8:30 a.m. in formal dining room with hostess and often host attired in colonial dress; depending upon season, a breakfast may include freshly baked muffins, sausage, sourdough griddle cakes, fruit, juice and beverages. Anniversary couples receive complimentary champagne. Guests will find packages of Lancaster candy in their rooms.

Extra Facilities & Features

Special weekend packages that include dinner and an evening at the Fulton Theater. Jan has a display of locally-made Amish quilts for sale.

Jan & Dick Kennell

33 E. Main St., Strasburg, PA 17579. Phone: (717) 687-8392; best to call 10 a.m. to 7 p.m. Location: Lancaster County, 3 miles south of Route 30 on Route 896.

MERCERSBURG
INN

ercersburg, nestled at the foot of the Tuscarora range of the Blue Ridge Mountains, played a role in every aspect of American history. This small village began as a trading center for settlers heading west across the mountains and was later named after physician Hugh Mercer, who had died at the Battle of Princeton in 1777. George Washington, upon Mercer's death, suggested that the town change its name from Smith's Town to Mercersburg in honor of his close friend.

The log cabin birthplace and boyhood home of President James Buchanan is located on what is today the campus of the Mercersburg Academy, a renowned secondary boarding school.

Eighty years ago a prominent local businessman, Harry Byron, with unlimited wealth and a vision for what was required to create a lifestyle of casual elegance, took nearly two years to create one of the town's landmarks, "Prospect," a six-acre estate which is now the Mercersburg Inn.

Built of brick with slate roof, Indiana limestone sills and lintels, copper spouting, tile and white oak flooring, wrought iron balustrades, marble columns and mahogany panelling, it endures today as a classic example of fine Georgian design. The fact that a regulation 88-foot bowling alley once was accommodated in the basement gives an idea of the immensity of this 21,000-square-foot mansion. Today that room is the game room for the guests.

Details

Check in: 2 p.m. Check out: 11 a.m. Deposit/Cancellation Policy: one night's stay sent ahead or credit card payment. Full refund with 14 days' notice. Payment: cash, personal check, MasterCard, VISA. Children welcome. Smoking permitted in designated areas. In residence: yellow Lab, Maggie, and teenage son, Nat. Handicap access to public dining room; guest rooms are on second and third floor. Phones in rooms. Air conditioning throughout the inn. Off-street parking.

Rates

$105 - $145. Room with king-size canopy bed, fireplace, and balcony $175. Roll-away $25. Best to call one month in advance for major and holiday weekends. Two-night minimum for October weekends and holidays — also for fireplace rooms in season.

Bed & Bath

Fifteen rooms, all with private bath and king, queen, double, or twin beds. Two rooms have working fireplaces and four have private balconies or porches. Furnished with nice selection of period antiques and down comforters. Most have king-size canopied beds. Three of the private baths are the original huge, luxurious 1909 bathrooms. Each of these has original tile throughout, two large porcelain tubs, others with separate marble shower, porcelain sitz bath, and commode.

Breakfast & Extras

Served in a sun room overlooking the town and mountains, a breakfast featuring home-baked breads, fresh fruit, spiced apple cider, spiced tomato juice, or freshly-squeezed orange juice and hot beverages. The Morel Restaurant is open for dinner Wednesday through Sunday. All organically-grown vegetables and fruits come from local farms. A la carte menu changes seasonally while six-course prix fixe menu changes nightly. Typical offering includes smoked sea scallops with light lemon curry sauce or roasted lamb with juniper berries and spatzle.

Extra Facilities & Features

Conference facilities include large parquet-floored banquet room suitable for 24 - 70 participants depending upon setup. Also two other small meeting rooms: Rose Room seats 12, and Sun Room seats 15 - 20. Both appropriate for break-out rooms with larger conference or as small business meeting rooms. Equipment available includes flip charts, overhead projector and screens, 35 mm slide projector and screen, VHS recorder and television. Meeting room fee is $75 per day. Also variety of business meeting packages addressing a wide range of needs. Request brochure listing corporate information and price ranges. Because of the double curving stairway and grand scale of the foyer and first floor, it is a popular place for weddings.

Fran Wolfe

405 S. Main St., Mercersburg, PA 17236. Phone: (717) 328-5231, 8 a.m. - 5 p.m. any day; answering machine other times. Location: Franklin County, off I-81, Exit 3, 12 minutes west on Route 16. Less than one hour from Gettysburg, Antietam, and Harper's Ferry. Two hours from Frank Lloyd Wright's Falling Water and Lancaster area.

MT. GRETNA INN

Travelers happening upon this tiny mountain village are often surprised to discover this quaint town is host to a thriving cultural community modeled after the late 1800s Chatauqua Movement. Each season brings some form of cultural event, with outdoor chamber concerts, jazz fests, music theater and art shows delighting summer visitors.

Serving as a quiet refuge on the town's only area of open land is a mansion, built in 1921 by a local entrepreneur who admired the clean, simple architectural style of Gustav Stickley, father of the American arts and crafts movement. Over the years the mansion has been a private home, church camp, bar and restaurant, and most recently, the elegant Mt. Gretna Inn.

Impeccably furnished with an eclectic mix of various styles popular in the late 19th- and early-20th centuries, the inn features pieces from the Fleta Plantation along the Mississippi in southern Louisiana. Once owned by Bill's great-grandfather, the plantation's beautiful mid-Victorian furnishings help complete a picture-perfect decor.

Bill, a native of Louisiana, treats guests to true Southern hospitality, with his congenial personality and casual manner making visitors feel welcome from the moment they cross the threshold.

To keep with the spirit of the community, guests are encouraged to bring their own instruments for impromptu evening performances around the parlor's baby grand.

Although the town itself has enough cultural activities to keep almost anyone occupied, only a short drive away are all of south central Pennsylvania's sites, including Dutch Country and Hershey's Chocolate World.

Details

Check in: 3 p.m. Check out: 11 a.m.
Deposit/Cancellation Policy: credit card
guarantee, refunded with ten days'
notice. Payment: cash, personal check,
MasterCard, VISA, or American
Express. Please no children. Smoking
permitted in designated areas only.
Unsuitable for guest pets. In residence:
Mr. Puttz, half dachshund and "half
short neighbor." No handicap access. Air
conditioning in guest rooms. Off-street
parking.

Rates

$95 - $125 double occupancy. $105 -
$125 suites. Additional $25 for extra
person in room. Best to call one - two
months in advance for peak and holiday
weekends. Two- or three-night
minimum stay on Saturdays and some
holidays.

Bed & Bath

Four guest rooms and four suites,
including a special honeymoon suite, all
with private bath in room. Two have
double jacuzzi baths and two have
private porches. Rooms contain mid-
Victorian antiques and most have
queen-size beds. All have fresh flowers,
Oriental rugs, and antique prints and
photo-graphs. Concierge service
provided.

Breakfast & Extras

Served fireside in the formal dining
room, a candlelit breakfast served on
fine china with silver and crystal
appointments while Mozart plays in the
background. The menu may include
cantaloupe with blueberries (or in-
season fruit), black raspberry cobbler
and Scottish griddle scones, fruit juice or
mimosa, and beverages. Tea and biscuits
offered each evening at 5:30 in parlor, or
weather permitting, on covered porch.
With advance notice, a romantic evening
dinner is available for additional charge.

Extra Facilities & Features

Space available for up to 16 persons
attending a conference. Fax available
nearby. Catering for lunch and dinner
can be arranged. Corporate rate. Half-
acre lawn is terraced down to a flat for
badminton and croquet. Tennis courts,
golf course, cross-country ski trails, and
lake for canoeing nearby.

Bill Cook

*Kauffman Avenue, Mt. Gretna, PA 17064.
Phone: (717) 964-3234, after 10 a.m.,
answering machine when not available.
Location: Lebanon County, off PA
Turnpike 76, Exit 20, continue 3 miles on
Route 72N, Exit 117, 2 miles to Mt. Gretna.*

SMITHTON INN

$\mathcal{J}$n June 1763, Henry Miller opened an inn and tavern to serve stagecoach travelers and visitors who came to see the famous Ephrata Cloister. Members of the Cloister, a Protestant monastic society founded in 1732, built a cloister of medieval German buildings that survive today as a much-visited museum.

A traveler's diary once noted that Henry Miller and his wife kept a good and proper house that would not offend a lady. Limits were imposed on how many could be lodged in one room or sleep in one bed.

The Miller house continued to operate as a public place until the Civil War. It was finally sold in the late 1970s after being in the same family for 200 years.

Now known as Smithton, the inn has changed little in ensuing years except for the additions of 20th-century amenities. Guests still enjoy it as a place offering matchless hospitality, where leisurely evenings are enjoyed before the fires in the great room and the library. Here the tradition of welcoming visitors to Lancaster County for weekend getaways or for a respite during cross-country journeys continues much as it did years ago. Smithton is a place where the list of extras is so long that innkeeper Dorothy Graybill says, "It would sound foolish trying to recite them all."

For first-time visitors to Lancaster County, Dorothy is an invaluable source of information. A native of Ephrata and about as Pennsylvania Dutch as a person can be, she's a veritable resource on Lancaster County's bewildering variety of activities and places to visit.

Details

Check in: 3:30 p.m. to 7:30 p.m. Check out: 12 noon. Deposit/Cancellation Policy: credit card guarantee or prepayment. Full refund is made if cancelled two weeks prior to reservation or if room is rebooked. Payment: cash, personal check, MasterCard, VISA, or American Express. Well-mannered children welcome. No smoking. Guest pets with advance permission only. Gold Room is handicap-accessible. Individual room air conditioning. Off-street parking.

Rates

$65 - $115 double occupancy. $140 - $170 for suite. Children: under 18 months free, under 12 years $20, over 11 years $35. Best to call six weeks in advance for major weekends. Saturday or holiday reservations require a two-night stay.

Bed & Bath

Seven meticulously restored and appointed rooms, plus a spacious four-room south-wing suite offering a large bedroom that sleeps three, parlor, snack area, and bath with whirlpool and shower. All rooms have their own working fireplace and can be candlelit during evening hours. Sitting area in each room has leather upholstered chairs, reading lamps and writing desk. Most beds have canopies, are double or queen-size, and feature Pennsylvania Dutch quilts and goose-down pillows. Feather beds upon request. Private baths in each room. The White Room has a claw-foot tub and the Red Room has a whirlpool. Rooms are provided with chamber music, a selection of books, Smithton's Suggestion Book and private refrigerators. Night shirts are available for guests to wear. Fresh flowers in every room, including bath.

Breakfast & Extras

Served in the dining room with its display of china and exquisite handmade and hand-painted furniture, which has been patterned after that found at the Cloister. Breakfast is an "all you can eat" affair that may include waffles, French toast, pancakes, fruit platter, pastries and coffee, tea and juice. The sideboard has a fresh supply of hot and cold beverages and pastries for guests to enjoy from 3:30 p.m. to 9:30 p.m.

Extra Facilities & Features

Telephone access available. Fax available. Children love the lop-ear bunnies raised at the inn and feeding the Koi fish in the pond. Families are welcome to try their hand at croquet. Grounds are expansive with extensive gardens and fruit trees – many in their original location.

Dorothy Graybill, *Innkeeper*

900 W. Main St., (Route 322), Ephrata, PA 17522. Phone: (717) 733-6094, best after 8 a.m. and before 10 p.m., answering machine other times. Location: Lancaster County, 11 miles north of Lancaster, 5 miles south of Turnpike. Follow Route 222 to Ephrata exit, then west on 322, 2 1/2 miles. Located at the top of the hill just above the Ephrata Cloister.

SWISS WOODS
BED &
BREAKFAST

hen Debbie left Pennsylvania in 1977, little did she know that she would meet her husband-to-be in Belgium. She and Swiss-born Werner were both there on missions for their churches.

After getting married, they settled in Switzerland until 1985, when they returned to Debbie's native Lancaster County.

On 30 acres of land that has been in her family for four decades, they have created an inn with a warm, personal setting, bringing a little bit of Switzerland to Pennsylvania, in Debbie's words, to help keep Werner from getting too homesick.

For anyone who has never had the pleasure of visiting Switzerland and the Swiss Alps, a visit to Swiss Woods certainly has the flavor of a fine country European inn.

Overlooking Speedwell Lake, their home has an overhanging roof with exposed beams, a massive sandstone fireplace that is the focal point of the common room, and Swiss bells and decorations everywhere. Outside on the 30 acres of woods and pastures, there are hiking and cross-country trails, opportunities for canoeing and fishing at the lake, plus wonderful sites for birdwatching.

Because of the Mosimanns' background, the hosts often arrange entire bed and breakfast tours of two to three weeks' duration throughout the East Coast for European travelers.

Details

Check in: 3 p.m. Check out: 11 a.m. Deposit/Cancellation Policy: $25 deposit per room per night or credit card guarantee. Refunded if canceled seven days prior to date. Payment: cash, personal check, MasterCard, or VISA. Children welcome. No smoking. Unsuitable for guest pets. Kennels 15 minutes away. In residence: four school- and toddler-age children, Mirjam, Esther, Lukas, and Jason. Two golden retrievers, Gretle and Heidi kept outside. No handicap access. Central air conditioning. Off-street parking.

Rates

$75 - $110. $15 for extra person in room. Best to call six to eight weeks in advance for weekend or holiday reservations. Two-night minimum stay weekends. Three-night minimum holidays.

Bed & Bath

Six guest rooms all with private bath in rooms, plus one suite. Four rooms have private terraces, three including the suite have a balcony. Two rooms offer jacuzzis. One guest room has two European-size twin beds, others have varying types of queen-size beds including canopies, four poster, and sleigh beds. The Matternhorn Suite is especially suited for families with its two large rooms containing a queen and twin bed, living room with pine furnishings, and queen sleeper sofa. Roll-away and crib also available. All guest rooms are bright and airy with European-style pine wood furnishings, large windows with varying views of gardens and countryside, and thick down comforters on all beds. Crabtree and Evelyn toiletries provided and fresh flowers in every room.

Breakfast & Extras

Served in an open country dining room boasting three large picture windows, a hearty Swiss breakfast of pears poached in raspberry sauce, egg-sausage souffle, upside-down cherry muffins, blueberry muffins with lemon curd, croissants and Swiss butter bread. Jellies, butters and cream cheeses are all homemade. Coffee beans are freshly ground each morning. Fully-equipped kitchen available just for guests. Swiss specialty dinners by reservation January through March.

Extra Facilities & Features

Common room suitable for business meetings and retreats. Seats up to 20. Catering for lunch and dinner can be arranged. Special corporate rate. Besides English, family speaks fluent German and Swiss German. Hiking and ski trails, fishing and canoeing on site.

Debrah & Werner Mosimann

500 Blantz Road, Lititz, PA 17543. Phone: (717) 627-3358 or (800) 594-8018, best to call 10 a.m. and 8:30 p.m.; answering machine other times. Location: Lancaster County, follow Route 501 North from Lancaster through Lititz, left 1 mile on Brubaker Valley to Lake, right on Blantz Road.

WALKABOUT
INN

The name Walkabout Inn betrays the Australian heritage of one of the owners. After searching all over the East Coast for the perfect home and location, the Masons purchased this charming 1925 22-room brick home, with its chestnut milled woodwork, Oriental rugs and Pennsylvania Dutch stenciling. They then left their home and employment by the Australian government in Washington, D.C.

The inn's name reflects Richard's goal to see the world. Walkabout is an Australian word that means to go about and discover new places. He has lived, worked, or trained in dozens of countries on all but three continents. Guests can experience their own walkabout while staying at the inn — embarking on a tour of the Amish countryside, historic sites, farm markets and country auctions. Before departing, many guests take advantage of the 30-minute video on Amish life that the Masons make available to guests.

At the end of a busy day, the Walkabout's large wrap-around porches with three porch swings are the perfect place to rest weary feet. There is also a formal English garden to stroll through on the manicured one-acre yard. If time permits, the backyard offers badminton and croquet for the adults and a swingset for the children, while the community park adjacent to the inn has hiking trails for the entire family. Local Amish crafts can be purchased from the on-site "Outback" gift shop.

Details

Check in: 2 p.m. Check out: 11 a.m.
Deposit/Cancellation Policy: one night's
deposit upon making reservations.
Special weekends and holiday packages
no refund unless room is rebooked.
Otherwise, three days' notice for full
refund. Payment: cash, personal check,
MasterCard, VISA, or American Express.
Well-behaved children welcome.
Smoking limited to designated areas;
pipes and cigars on porches only.
Unsuitable for guest pets. Kennels
nearby. In residence: three children,
Nicholas, Megan and Geoffrey. Cable
television in rooms. No handicap access.
Central air conditioning. Off-street
parking.

Rates

$49 - $79 double occupancy. $150 for
suites (up to five persons). $15 for extra
person in room. Sunday through
Thursday two-night special rate. Inquire
about special honeymoon and
anniversary packages that include
Pennsylvania Dutch dinner and guided
tours of area. Also holiday specials
offered. If paying with credit card for
special packages, add additional 10%.
For holiday weekends and October
weekends, best to call several months in
advance. Two-night minimum these
times.

Bed & Bath

Five guest rooms. Four with private bath
in room, one with private bath in hall.
Quilt Room has double carved-oak bed
and antique fainting sofa with balcony
and porch swing. Lilac Room has canopy
double bed and single beds with
connecting living room and bath. The
Quilt and Strawberry Rooms or
Strawberry and Lilac Rooms can be
rented as suites. All rooms have
stenciled walls, Oriental carpets, antique
furnishings and hand-sewn quilts.

Breakfast & Extras

Served in formal dining room at one of
several finely-appointed tables, a hearty
country breakfast that includes freshly-
baked Australian tea ring, grapefruit
with kiwi and strawberries, country
sausage, cheddar cheese quiche, tropical
juices, and coffee or imported Australian
tea. High tea is served in late afternoons
on wrap-around porch or in parlor,
featuring scones and cream cheese,
cucumber sandwiches, sausage rolls,
Aussie meats, a selection of pastries and,
of course, Australian and English teas.
There is an additional charge and open
to the public.

Extra Facilities & Features

Meeting space available for up to ten
persons. Catering for lunch and dinner
can be arranged. 10% corporate
discount. Dinner can be arranged with a
local Amish family. Three-hour tours of
area that pick up and drop off at inn can
be arranged.

Richard & Margaret Mason

*837 Village Road, Box 294, Lampeter, PA
17537. Phone: (717) 464-0707, best to call
2 - 10 p.m., answering machine other times.
Location: Lancaster County, 3 miles south
of the city of Lancaster, in village of Lampeter
on Route 741, 2 miles west of Strasburg.*

GENERAL EVANS INN

In 1805 when the sheriff brought down the gavel for the last time, Louis Evans became the new owner of property that was originally part of a land grant from William Penn.

The War of 1812 interrupted construction of the Federal-style stone mansion as Evans saw service as a brigadier general. Upon his return, the final stages were influenced by the various architectural styles he became familiar with during his travels. Among the special features found throughout the inn is the extensive use of chestnut woodwork.

Today, guests contemplate days gone by as they lounge on the wraparound porch or in front of the fireplace.

With Darlene's western Canadian origins and Doug's New Mexico background, the hosts' personalities combine to bring a special flair and hospitality to this inn.

Details

Check in: flexible. Check out: 11 a.m. - negotiable. Deposit/Cancellation Policy: 50% of total stay sent in advance, full refund less $10 processing fee for cancellations 14 days or more in advance, prior to seven days, 50% refund if room rented. Less than seven days, forfeited. Payment: personal check. No credit cards. Children over 4 welcome. No smoking. Three friendly, outside only, Labrador retrievers. No handicap access. Air conditioning downstairs. Window fans in guest rooms.

Rates

$60 double occupancy.

Bed & Bath

Three guest rooms, one with an adjoining room used when a family of four travels together. Shared bath. Antique double beds and period furnishings, lace accents, Amish quilts, stenciled floors, fresh flowers and mints on pillows.

Breakfast & Extras

Served in formal dining room a breakfast that includes fresh fruit, muffins, scones, cereal, juice and beverages. Freshly-baked cookies, tarts and beverages set out for afternoon or evening snack.

Extra Facilities & Features

Four acres of lush countryside surrounded by dairy farms, many Amish-owned. Nearby hiking trails and fishing.

Doug Blagg & Darlene Wilke

R. D. #1, Box 5, Thompsontown, PA 17094. Phone: (717) 535-5678, best to call evenings, answering machine other times. Location: Juniata County, 1/8 mile from Route 322 on Route 333 towards East Salem. Five minutes from Ski Snow Peak and ten minutes from Buffalo State Park.

In the mid-1800s when the first section of this white clapboard farmhouse was built, Pine Grove Mills was a quiet farming community situated at the base of Tussey Mountain. Little has changed. The white clapboard house still sits on a tree-lined property just outside of town with an unchanging, spectacular view of Tussey Mountain.

The artfully decorated home equals Mae's southern-style hospitality and charm. Well-traveled, her family settled in Pine Grove Mills many years ago. Mae says ". . . the world comes to me for rest and peace. This is truly a creative outlet for me."

SPLIT PINE FARMHOUSE

Details

Check in: 10 a.m. Check out: 3 p.m. Deposit/Cancellation Policy: $20 per room per night. Refund seven days prior, 14 days if peak weekend. Payment: cash, personal check, MasterCard, or VISA. No smoking, inside. Well-behaved children over 8 welcome. In residence: one cat, Pusskins, and occasionally one "granddog" Delta. Unsuitable for guest pets. Kennels nearby. No handicap access. Window fans in guest rooms when necessary. Off-street parking.

Rates

$58 - $68 double occupancy. $8 one night surcharge on peak Penn State weekends. Also option to book one room for $80 to guarantee private bath.

Bed & Bath

Three antique-filled, elegantly appointed guest rooms, with king or queen beds; share two baths.

Breakfast & Extras

Served in the formal dining room where heirloom mahogany and a handmade painted corner cupboard create gracious ambiance. The buffet typically features Smithfield ham, poppyseed Danish home-baked popovers, gooseberry compote with mascarpone, pineapple juice, and Scandinavian coffee. Each guest room has table and chairs which can be set for a romantic breakfast with advance notice. Afternoon refreshments of soft drinks, iced coffee, or tea are available to enjoy while relaxing by the fireplace or outside on the patio. Guests will find bedside cordials at night.

Ida Mae McQuade

Box 326, Pine Grove Mills, PA 16868. Phone: (814) 238-2028, best after 6 p.m. Location: Centre County, about 6 miles west of State College and Penn State on Route 45.

BLUE LION INN

Snyder County's oldest and largest sugar maple tree, predating even William Penn, presides over the grounds of this 150-year-old plantation home. When John Witmer was granted 166 acres by the state of Pennsylvania in 1814, it would have already been a mature tree providing shade to the new settlers. In 1847, a surveyor, who later was a colonel in the Civil War, purchased the property from the Witmers, with the deed reading, "166 acres 154 perches (a unit of measure), a plantation with all dwellings, houses thereon." One of these houses was a brick structure, considerably smaller than it is now and currently known as the Blue Lion Inn. Over the years, several additions were made, outbuildings were constructed, and remodeling and restoration work was completed. Its varied history includes use as a state police barracks, a private home and now the delightful Blue Lion Inn.

The Thomsons, with their outstanding hospitality and careful restoration, have managed to recreate an atmosphere reminiscent of a more gracious, relaxed era. The home's colorful history is reflected in the choice of period furnishings and appointments. Besides providing a relaxing atmosphere for reading and afternoon tea, the library is a perfect place for a game of cards or maybe chess. The parlor with its fireplace and all the latest in electronic equipment often becomes a lively evening gathering place, where guests get to know each other and parents of university students trade stories.

Details

Check in: 2 - 6 p.m. Check out: 11 a.m. Deposit/Cancellation Policy: 25% deposit two weeks prior to stay, refundable with five days' notice prior to reservation. Payment: cash, personal check, MasterCard, VISA, or American Express. Children 6 and older welcome. No smoking. Unsuitable for guest pets. Kennels nearby. No handicap access. No air conditioning, ceiling fans in rooms. Off-street parking.

Rates

$52.50 - $62.50 double occupancy. $75 - $105 suites. $10 for additional person in room. Best to call several weeks in advance for major college weekends. Two-night minimum stay during Parents and Homecoming weekends.

Bed & Bath

Three guest rooms with private baths, plus two adjoining rooms that serve as a spacious suite with own bath or when rented individually, a shared bath. Individual themes and decors range from the Jade Room's Oriental motif to the Sleigh Room's antique oak sleigh bed. Jade Room also has jacuzzi tub/ shower combination. Special toiletries, fresh flowers, fruit baskets and an amenity basket filled with oft-forgotten items welcome guests arrival in each room. An upstairs sitting room and small porch provide a quiet refuge.

Breakfast & Extras

Served in formal dining room, garden room, colonial keeping room, or weather permitting, garden gazebo, a filling breakfast that may include an apple Brie omelette with ham, fresh fruit, homemade buns, choice of juices and beverages. Guests may enjoy afternoon refreshments on wrap-around porch or in spacious parlor. Evenings find wine and snacks being served in the library. Wedding couples are served a champagne breakfast in their room.

Extra Facilities & Features

Library offers business meetings space for up to ten persons. Catering for lunch and dinner can be arranged. Special corporate rate. The Garden Gazebo provides romantic setting for weddings

Kent & Marilyn Thomson

350 S. Market St., Selinsgrove, PA 17870. Phone: (717) 374-2929, best to call 10 a.m. - 9 p.m.; answering machine other times. Location: Snyder County, 50 miles north of Harrisburg on Routes 11 and 15, 20 miles south of I-80 Exits 30 or 33. Several blocks from Susquehanna University and convenient to Bucknell and Penn State universities.

BODINE HOUSE

To offer a safe haven for white settlers, Fort Brady and Fort Muncy were established at the site of the Indian ancestral home of the Wolf Clan's Minsi tribe. In the late 1700s, land grants were issued by John Penn and as new landholders moved in, the Minsi tribe was gradually pushed westward. During this period the former Indian path became the Great Road, and today it is the Main Street where the Bodine House Bed & Breakfast greets passersby.

Over the years, the 1805 post-and-beam framed house has witnessed many changes in this charming 1800s canal town. The colorful local history is reflected in the numerous occupations and businesses that have been housed in this two-story Federal-style townhouse.

Just three blocks from the town center, the current owners, David and Marie Louise, state, "When you come to town, be prepared to step back in time." Muncy, as well as the Bodine House, are listed on the National Register of Historic Places. Homeowners all take great pride in their homes.

Over the years, interior changes at Bodine were minor and retained the authentic colonial decor. During the recent restoration process, four fireplaces were re-opened to warm guests during chilly winter months, especially after a busy day of cross-country skiing or tobogganing, popular activities in the area.

Nearby, several state parks offer swimming and hiking. Antique shops and the famous Woolrich Woolen Mills outlet store welcome travelers year around.

Details

Check in: 2 p.m. Check out: 10:30 a.m. Deposit/Cancellation Policy: one night's stay deposit, refunded if cancelled five days prior to reservation. Payment: cash, personal check, MasterCard, VISA, or American Express. Children over 6 welcome. Smoking outside only. Unsuitable for guest pets. No handicap access. Individual room air conditioning. Off-street parking.

Rates

$55 - $65 double occupancy. $80 - $100 for Carriage House. $10 extra person in room. Roll-away cots available. Best to call several weeks in advance for peak university and ski weekends. Two-night minimum stay during January, February and October weekends.

Bed & Bath

Four guest rooms, two with private bath and two share a hall bath (with restored claw-foot tub), also a separate Carriage House Suite with two bedrooms. Altland Room has double canopy bed and private bath; Repplier Room has two twin pencil-post beds, private bath, and fireplace; Prescott Room with double pencil-post bed has one-half bath and shares full bath with Chaffee Room, which has double bed. The Carriage House is a two-floor suite; ground level has queen-size bed with bath; second floor has two twin beds. Rooms are tastefully furnished with selection of antiques dating from 1750 to 1840 and appropriate reproductions. Quilts, wall hangings and other appropriate accessories complete the historic atmosphere of the rooms.

Breakfast & Extras

Served fireside during winter months in what was once the original house kitchen, or outside in 18th-century courtyard and gardens, a breakfast of cereal, eggs, bacon, French toast, muffins, rolls, jellies, juice and beverages. Wine and cheese is offered in parlor from 5 to 7 p.m. each evening.

Extra Facilities & Features

Space available for small meetings of up to ten participants. Catering for lunch and dinner can be arranged. Special corporate rate. Several bicycles available for touring the countryside. Guests may play badminton and croquet on manicured back lawn.

David & Mary Louise Smith

307 S. Main St., Muncy, PA 17756. Phone: (717) 546-8949, anytime; if not available, answering machine takes message. Location: Lycoming County, use I-80 Exit 31-B to I-180 to Muncy Main Street Exit, left 1 mile to inn.

INN AT TURKEY HILL

*O*riginally designed as a private residence in 1839, this white brick farmhouse was bought by the Eyerly family in 1942, and for 40 years it was the home that Babs Eyerly Pruden played in as a child and visited as a Maryland housewife.

Then in 1982, she decided to help her dad, Paul, make his longtime dream a reality, creating a distinctive country inn worthy of a four-diamond AAA award.

Her father, president of the Bloomsburg newspaper, died two months before construction began. Thus for Babs, "the project," as she calls it, became as much of a tribute to him as a business for herself.

Construction entailed building a charming complex of country cottages for the majority of the guest rooms, while converting the family kitchen and family room into the lobby and tavern. Two of the three dining rooms are in the main house as are two of the guest rooms. The front part of the home retained the shuttered windows and Victorian porch, looking much as it did when Babs was a child. A recent addition has been attached in back. New landscaping enhances the ancient maples guarding the property, and an informal courtyard with duck pond and gazebo completes the tranquil scene.

The inn is now managed by her son Andrew. The continuous attention to detail that earned them the coveted Four Diamond award from AAA is why many of their guests return again and again.

Details

Check in: 2 p.m. Check out: 12 noon. Deposit/Cancellation Policy: credit card guarantee, not charged within 24 hours' notice. $40 fee for no-shows. Payment: cash, personal check, MasterCard, VISA, American Express, Diners Club, Discover, or Carte Blanche. Children welcome. Smoking permitted in designated areas. Guest pets permitted. Handicap access with exterior ramps. Central air conditioning. Off-street parking.

Rates

$68 - $90 double occupancy. $145 suites. $15 extra person in room. Sleeping bags permitted - extra charge applies. Use of cot or crib, $10. Each pet, $15.

Bed & Bath

Sixteen rooms and two suites, all with private bath. The white clapboard complex of country cottages form a semi-circle, holding 14 oversize rooms and two suites. The main house has two rooms, one with a queen-size bed and jacuzzi while the other has a king-size bed and private bath. The suites each have a working fireplace and a double jacuzzi. Furnishings in all rooms include handmade reproductions from Georgia's Habersham Plantation, each piece signed and dated. Beds have European duvets and down pillows. Toiletries in the bath. Decor is in Williamsburg colors complemented by country primitive oil paintings by a local artist. Remote-control televisions and phones in all rooms. Each cottage room overlooks the informal courtyard and the duck pond; a profusion of flowers surrounds the white-latticed gazebo and groomed paths for morning strolls.

Breakfast & Extras

Served in the glass-enclosed greenhouse, a breakfast of assorted muffins, bagels, fresh fruit, juice; and beverages. A complimentary local or national newspaper accompanies the meal. Breakfast in a country basket will be delivered to the room upon request. Sundays feature a delicious brunch. Dinner available in one of three dining rooms, open to inn guests and the public. The Mural Room is one of two formal dining areas with scenes of Pennsylvania countryside painted on the walls. The less formal Greenhouse Dining Room overlooks the duck pond and gazebo. It is a favorite at night when guests can enjoy their meals under a star-filled sky. Menu is varied and balanced offering such diverse fare as capellini with spicy fennel sausage in cream sauce, rabbit marinated in burgundy and sauteed with fresh herbs, or duck stuffed with wild rice, walnuts and raisins, bathed in a tangy ligonberry sauce.

Extra Facilities & Features

Conference space available for 15 - 20 participants. Indoor and outdoor facilities available for weddings and receptions. On holidays, special amenities are offered including special sweets on Valentine's Day and Santa's Stocking hung on guests' doors Christmas morning.

Andrew Pruden, Innkeeper
Elizabeth Pruden, Owner

991 Central Road, Bloomsburg, PA 17815. Phone: (717) 387-1500, 8 a.m. - 3 p.m. 24 hours a day. Location: Columbia County, just off I-80 Exit 35, 1 mile from Bloomsburg University, 15 minutes from Ricketts Glen State Park.

PINEAPPLE INN

German immigrant Lewis Derr bought 320 prime acres near the Susquehanna in 1772 and proceeded to open a mill and Indian trading post. With the success of this venture he began laying out a town that 80 years later became so prosperous it was established as the county seat. Mr. Derr's town, Lewisburg, attracted an eminent architect, Louis Palmer. In 1857 Mr. Palmer was commissioned to design an elegant Federal-style brick home, which he built alongside numerous other prominent buildings on the bustling main street of this quaint village.

Nearly 120 years later, Charles North was serving as convention director of the Washington, D.C., Hilton. He handled the media the day President Reagan was shot while leaving the hotel, and thereafter decided the time had come to fulfill a long-time dream of finding some quiet little undiscovered town and opening an inn.

Parenthood finally prompted the Norths to make their dream a reality. Happening upon the 19th-century town of Lewisburg and Louis Palmer's carefully restored home, they have never looked back.

Named for the hospitality it extends to all visitors, Pineapple Inn is an anomaly combining Victorian furnishings, equestrian artifacts, brass rubbings, and authentic furniture of the Archbishop of Canterbury. It also reflects Deborah's background in Middle East archeology, religion and philosophy.

Located a few short blocks from Bucknell University, the inn gives vistors easy access to Lewisburg and its plethora of activities. Besides the countless antique shops, speciality stores and recreational opportunities, there are many unique museums offering glimpses into every facet of 19th-century life.

Details

Check in: 4 p.m. Check out: noon. Deposit/Cancellation Policy: one night's lodging sent or credit card guarantee. Refunded with five days' notice; 14 day's notice required on peak college weekends. Payment: cash, personal check, MasterCard, VISA, American Express, Diners, or Carte Blanche. Well-behaved and supervised children of all ages welcome. Smoking permitted in parlor. Unsuitable for guest pets. Kennels nearby. In residence: elementary school-age children, Marisa, Chad, and Chris. Central air conditioning. No handicap access. Limited off-street parking. Safe, daytime metered parking on side street next to inn. No charge for overnight parking.

Rates

$59 - $79 double occupancy. $90 - $130 suites. $15 cot. Best to call up to six months in advance for area colleges' peak weekends. Two-night minimum these events.

Bed & Bath

Six rooms; two with private bath in room, four share two baths. The Canterbury Room contains antique bedroom suite belonging to one Arch-bishop of Canterbury, has queen-size brass bed, private bath with clawfoot tub, shower. The Blue Willow Room has two twin sleigh beds, private bath has locally hand-painted "Blue Willow" design tiles, large shower with inset seat and easy on/off faucets for older guests. Other rooms include the Country Room with full-size 1810 rope bed and shares bath with the Canterbury Room if booked as a suite, or on its own, shares bath with Tree of Life Room with 1870 sleigh bed. The Washington Room with queen-size brass bed shares bath with the Currier and Ives Room with two twin beds. Generally, these two rooms are booked as a family suite or by folks traveling together. The suite features a stairway entrance from dining room, affording a quiet and private guest area. All rooms have period antiques, hand-made quilts.

Breakfast & Extras

Served in formal dining room, a full breakfast that will variably include Amish slab-cut bacon; country fresh brown eggs; Amish whole wheat, white, or raisin breads; Walnut Acres granolas; cottage cheese pancakes served with local honey, apple butter, jams; apple cider and beverages. Home-grown mint iced tea served warm summer afternoons. Locally-made pineapple-shaped chocolates offered.

Extra Facilities & Features

Space available for small business meetings up to ten. Fax available. Phones in some rooms. Sitting Room features an office atmosphere for corporate guests. It has touch-tone phone, desk space, television, coffee maker, refrigerator and ample privacy. Catering possible. Will host small wedding receptions and bridal teas. On-site gift shop, Upside-Downe Shoppe, features crafts and antiques of the Susquehanna Valley.

Charles & Deborah North

439 Market St., Lewisburg, PA 17837. Phone: (717) 524-6200, 10 a.m. - 10 p.m., answering machine other times. Location: Union County, 9 miles off I-80 Exit 30-A, follow Route 15 South, left 45 East (Market Street), 4 blocks. Bucknell University is 6 blocks away.

REST & REPAST
R S O

Early settlers in Central Pennsylvania found the area rich in limestone and iron ore, which resulted in Bellefonte becoming a center for the iron industry. Prosperity during the 1800s is reflected in the numerous ornate Victorian buildings. Home to seven governors, Bellefonte had political influence throughout the East Coast.

As the iron industry grew, so did the village surrounding Roland Curtin's "Eagle Forge" and Furnace. In 1836 he decided to move from Bellefonte and build a large mansion on land that would become the center of Curtin Village.

Today, a modern log home sits atop a wooded knoll, looking down upon the historic village. Visitors staying here can pack a picnic lunch, walk to the historic village, tour the restored Eagle Iron works and Curtin mansion, and later enjoy a train ride into Victorian Bellefonte. During summer weekends, the Bellefonte Historical Railroad Society schedules regular runs through the valley to Bellefonte, Curtin, and Mill Hall. Nearby are Penn State University and Bald Eagle State Park, which has boat launches, swimming facilities, and a stocked lake for fishing.

At Curtinview, B & B guests are welcome to relax and enjoy the incredible scenery from the large front porch. Besides the scenic view of the Allegheny foothills, particularly breathtaking in the fall, guests delight in watching the variety of wildlife come out of hiding for their evening meal.

Details

Check in: after 3 p.m. Check out: 10:30 a.m. Deposit/CancellationPolicy: refunds less $20 processing fee if cancellations made 14 days prior to date. Payment: cash or personal check. Children over 12 welcome. No smoking inside. No guest pets. Kennels nearby. In residence: three cats, Midnight, Tabatha and Wooley, and a springer spaniel. No handicap access. Air conditioning in guest rooms available if necessary; bedrooms have ceiling fans. Off-street parking.

Rates

$50 double occupancy. $10 one-night surcharge on peak weekends if two-night minimum is waived. Children with own sleeping bag $15. Roll-away $20. If entire area is booked with one group, the optional sofa bed available in common room is $25. Two-night minimum during most peak Penn State weekends.

Bed& Bath

When the home was built in 1989, hosts, who are experienced B & B travelers, designed this area for guests' comfort. It features a two-bedroom suite with guest bath and a common sitting area with sofa and television, all on a private second floor loft. Bedrooms have cathedral ceilings with fans. Larger room has two twin beds, smaller room has antique rope bed modified for a standard double mattress. Rooms can be rented individually or as a unit.

Breakfast & Extras

Served in dining room or on outside deck, weather permitting, a continental plus breakfast of fresh fruit (in season), yogurt, cereal, muffins or French toast, juice and hot beverages. Welcoming glass of wine offered upon evening arrival.

Extra Facilities & Features

Hiking and cross-country ski trails on hosts' 20 wooded acres and on nearby state park lands. The host, a licensed pilot, has restored a 1947 Stinson airplane that he is happy to take interested guests to see if time permits.

Curtinview

For reservations contact: Rest & Repast Bed & Breakfast Reservation Service, Box 126, Pine Grove Mills, PA 16868. Phone: (814) 238-1484, mornings best, but anytime to leave message. Location: Centre County, walking distance to Curtin Village, off Route 150, 2 miles from I-80 Exit 23. 25 minutes from Penn State University.

REST & REPAST
R S O

Even before guests step out of their car, they will hear Pee Pee the duck, waddling over to make their acquaintance. Perhaps visitors who came calling during the early 19th century were greeted in much the same manner before stepping down from their buggy.

Certainly with the prominence and significant wealth of James Potter, Jr., and later William Allison, one can imagine the stature of visitors that came to meet with these influential gentlemen.

In a quiet valley, surrounded by the Alleghenies, these owners created an imposing three-story brick mansion that illustrates the merging of basic Georgian features with later ornate Victorian influences.

Today as guests wander around the 13 acres of fields and woods, there are reminders of the activities that once were part of life at this farm complex.

Several outbuildings, unbroken contours of millraces, stone culverts and portions of foundations all serve as visual evidence of the families' successful tanning and milling enterprises.

Horses graze the fields and sometimes have company in the back pasture where Sinking Creek attracts avid fly fisherman who try to outsmart the native trout.

The meticulously restored home incorporates a tasteful selection of imported period furnishings and reproduction pieces. The formal parlor can be used for small wedding receptions and intimate business meetings.

Details

Check in: 6 p.m. weekdays, after 1 p.m. weekends. Check out: 10:30 a.m. Deposit/Cancellation Policy: Refunds less $20 processing fee if cancellations made 14 days prior to date. Payment: cash or personal check. Children welcome if own sleeping bag provided. No smoking or guest pets. In residence: toddler Alyson; black Lab, Bear, and golden retriever, Holly. No air conditioning but floor fans available when necessary. Off-street parking.

Rates

$50 - $70 double occupancy per room depending upon season and room booked. Children with own sleeping bag $15. Two-night minimum stay on peak Penn State weekends. Best to call several months in advance for these weekends.

Bed & Bath

Four guest rooms. Blue room with pencil poster queen-size bed and Allison Room with double antique bed and fireplace, private baths in room. Lincoln Room with two twins and Peach Room with queen-size sleigh bed normally share a hallway bath. Lincoln and Allison Room share a common door and can be booked as a suite for families with children, using Allison Room bath. All rooms have period and reproduction furnishings, some of which are for sale.

Breakfast & Extras

Served fireside in formal dining room, a generous breakfast of freshly-baked scones or bread, a hot entree such as Belgian waffles, juice, fresh fruit and beverages. On weekends, guests are often treated to warm home-baked cookies.

General Potter Farm

For reservations contact: Rest & Repast Bed & Breakfast Reservation Service, Box 126, Pine Grove Mills, PA 16868. Phone: (814) 238-1484, mornings best, but anytime to leave message. Location: Centre County, 11 miles east of Penn State off Route 322 in Potters Mills.

REST & REPAST
R S O

$\mathfrak{G}$uests staying at the Willows have the advantage of not only enjoying a delightful Colonial Revival home, but also finding themselves within walking distance of the quaint village of Boalsburg, founded in 1808 by Scottish-Irish immigrants.

This 1870s white frame farmhouse, hidden amidst the pine trees, is all that remains of what used to be a 19th-century farm located on the outskirts of the village. Now, instead of cows across the street, there is a large park with a jogging trail, picnic areas and a small stream that meanders through the property.

Guests are greeted in a large country kitchen, and if time permits, welcomed with a nightcap in the large living room with its walk-in stone fireplace.

After breakfast, it is not uncommon for guests to wander outside and enjoy the gardens. They like to pause on the bridge to watch the native trout dart after waterbugs and leap for flies.

The nearby village of Boalsburg is a typical colonial town with two unique features. The folks of Boalsburg claim their town is the rightful birthplace of Memorial Day because their earlier citizens first decorated veterans' graves in 1864, five years prior to the U.S. government's passing of the official ordinance.

In addition, Boalsburg is the site of the Boal Estate which houses an authentic 16th-century Spanish chapel inherited and imported by the Boals in 1909 from the family of Christopher Columbus. The Columbus Chapel contains an admiral's desk that belonged to Christopher himself, as well as centuries-old European art and religious relics.

Details

Check in: 5 p.m. Monday through Friday; anytime by prior arrangement on weekends. Check out: 10:30 a.m. Deposit/Cancellation Policy: $20 per room per night, except peak weekends which is $40. Refund, less processing fee seven days prior to reservation and 14 days prior for peak weekend reservations. Payment: cash or personal checks. No credit cards. Well-behaved children over 12 welcome. No smoking inside. In residence: one cat, Miss Kitty, primarily kept outside. Unsuitable for guest pets. Kennels nearby. No handicap access. Floor fans can be provided for rooms when necessary. Off-street parking.

Rates

$45 - $70 double occupancy. $10 one night surcharge on peak weekends. Some two-night minimum stays on peak weekends.

Bed & Bath

Three guests rooms, furnished with family heirlooms and auction finds. Two rooms each have one double bed; one room has one double bed and one single bed. Share two baths. Upstairs bath with clawfoot tub was formerly a trunk closet.

Breakfast & Extras

Served either in the colonial dining room or, when weather permits, on the enclosed sun porch. Weekday guests are offered an ample "do-it-yourself" continental breakfast while weekend guests typically enjoy French toast Grand Marnier, eggs and sausage, fruit of the season, juice, beverages. Newlyweds spending their honeymoon with the Willows will find a split of champagne in their rooms. Guests arriving in the evening are offered a glass of wine to unwind from a busy day.

The Willows

For reservations contact: Rest & Repast Bed & Breakfast Reservation Service, Box 126, Pine Grove Mills, PA 16868. Phone: (814) 238-1484, mornings best for personal contact but anytime to leave a message. Location: Centre County, walking distance to Colonial Boalsburg, off Route 322, about 3 miles east of State College and Penn State.

Remember when Mom and Dad took the youngsters to visit Auntie's house, where the food was always just right, the bedrooms looked like they should be in a storybook, and Auntie always treated everyone extra special? Carmella and Allan have recreated that atmosphere for their bed and breakfast guests.

Having lived two years in Germany and visited many bed and breakfasts all over Europe, they decided upon retirement to open their home to guests.

Located on a quiet tree-lined street, Auntie M's affords an ideal home base for visitors looking for a slow-paced country town setting. Wellsboro's quaint gas-lit boulevards, well-kept homes, and peaceful atmosphere are surrounded by nearly limitless recreational opportunities, including the famous Pennsylvania Grand Canyon.

AUNTIE M'S

Allan & Camella Rupert

3 Sherwood St., Wellsboro, PA 16901. Phone: (717) 724-5771, best to call mornings and evenings, answering machine other times. Location: Tioga County, follow Route 6 to Main Street and heart of Wellsboro, minutes from Pennsylvania Grand Canyon.

ALLEGHENY FOREST

Details

Check in 3 p.m. Check out: 11 a.m. Deposit/Cancellation Policy: $25 deposit per room. Refunded with four days' notice. Payment: cash or personal check. Unsuitable for children and guest pets. No smoking inside. Kennels nearby. No handicap access. Ceiling and window fans in rooms.

Rates

$45 double occupancy. $60 suite. Two-night minimum stay on holiday weekends.

Bed & Bath

Three rooms available at any one time with shared baths. The Governor's Suite, with canopied king-sized bed and priviate bath is available by special request. It is the room that Governor and Mrs. Casey used while visiting Wellsboro during the Capital for A Day program. An upstairs small reading room with TV & VCR is open to all guests.

Breakfast & Extras

Served in a formal dining room, a breakfast featuring Virgin Marys, fresh pineapple wedge with kiwi, orange-pistachio French toast, pineapple-shaped ham slice, pineapple-carrot-pecan bread and beverages. Carmella is often busy whipping up one of her old-fashioned cookie recipes; accompanied with flavored coffee or lemonade, served in the parlor or on the patio.

Extra Facilities & Features

Golf packages offered include room, breakfast, dinner, greens fees and golf cart. Collectors Gift Shoppe features Allan's handcarved duck decoys, kaleidoscopes, and stained-glass originals.

CLARION RIVER LODGE

hirty years ago a wealthy Cleveland attorney forsook crowds and civilization to seek the most quiet, secluded piece of property he could locate in the great forests of Western Pennsylvania. He proceeded to develop a rustic private estate, including a home that featured native cut stone, wood paneling, oak beams, cathedral ceilings, and a massive stone fireplace. In 1986, the current owners purchased it; they converted the original home into the now-spacious lobby and dining areas and added 20 modern guest rooms.

The Clarion River Lodge, which is literally "over the river and through the woods," rivals some of the country's better-known nature destinations, especially during fall foliage season.

The gentle Clarion River passes within a stone's throw of the lodge. Cook Forest State Park, site of the largest remaining stand of virgin pine and hemlock in the East, surrounds the lodge and offers an endless selection of outdoor activities.

The lodge can arrange for canoes to be rented for a leisurely trip down the river. Outdoor activities at the lodge and Cook Forest include over 27 miles of cross-country ski and hiking trails, two bridle trails, picnic facilities, and excellent fishing. There is swimming, snowmobiling, hunting, skating and sledding in designated areas.

Clarion River Lodge is an ideal place to spend a wilderness weekend — no noise, or crowds, just a quiet romantic setting with acres and acres of woods and the Clarion River to explore.

Details

Check in: 2:00 p.m. Check out: noon. Deposit/Cancellation Policy: $50 to hold reservation. Full refund with 14 days notice, partial refund with seven days notice. Payment: cash, personal check, MasterCard, VISA, or American Express. Children over 12 welcome. Smoking is permitted throughout lodge. Unsuitable for guest pets. Limited handicap access to guest rooms. Some hiking trails at Cook Forest are paved so wheelchairs are negotiable. Central air conditioning. Off-street parking.

Rates

$57 - $99 double occupancy. $15 for extra person in room. Minimum two-night stay on weekends and holidays. Best to call two months in advance for holiday weekends.

Bed & Bath

Twenty guest rooms each with private bath in room. 16 rooms with queen -size bed, four with king. Each has own television, telephone, and a small refrigerator — great to store a picnic lunch. The clean simple lines of Danish furnishings help create a bright airy feeling. The "Ends" guest rooms have either a private deck or balcony. All have a great view of wooded countryside.

Breakfast & Extras

A continental breakfast of fresh fruit, pastries, breads and juice is served in the large country dining room. For folks with a larger morning appetite, a cooked breakfast is an option for a modest additional charge. Widely-acclaimed, full-service restaurant for lunch and dinner: chef-prepared menu choices and extensive wine selection.

Extra Facilities & Features

Space available for up to 40 participants for corporate retreats or conferences. Fax available. Special corporate rates apply. Wedding receptions and private parties for up to 75. Inquire about special weekend packages. Depending upon season, horse and buggy or sleigh rides available some weekends. Terrific canoeing; rentals available. Lodge has 1000 feet of river frontage.

Skip & Barbara Williams,
Innkeepers
John Brandon & Skip Williams, Owners

Box 150, Cooksburg, PA 16217. Phone: (800) 648-6743, anytime. Location: Forest County, off I-80 Exit 15, north on Route 36, 15 miles to Clarion River. After bridge turn right onto River Road, continue for 5 2/10 miles. Lodge driveway is on the left and is well marked.

GATEWAY LODGE

𝕴n 1681 King Charles II of England gave to William Penn a large tract of land that became known as the Black Forest. After 300 years, remnants of this primeval forest still remain, comprising Cook Forest. The white pines that were saplings during King Charles' reign now tower 200 feet with diameters exceeding three feet. Cecil B. deMille chose this pristine area for the site of his movie "Unconquered," the saga about the siege of Fort Pitt, starring Gary Cooper and Boris Karloff.

On the edge of this unspoiled setting is the Gateway Lodge, built as a rustic log cabin in 1934. Designed to harmonize with the forest, the lodge is constructed of pine and hemlock logs with wormy chestnut walls and trim, oak floors and thick beamed ceilings. Except for the front porch, indoor pool, and added staircase, the lodge stands as it was originally built.

From the log walls and weathered stone fireplace in the Great Room to the big front porch with its wicker furniture and porch swing, Gateway Lodge offers the perfect rustic setting for an escape from civilization. Surrounded by Cook Forest, recreational activities are abundant year-round, with visitors enjoying everything from birdwatching to inner-tubing to horseback riding to ice skating.

Call early for reservations! The Burneys have created an inn known for its attention to detail, hospitality and excellent food. The attentive staff follows Linda's motto that there are no unimportant jobs here — an attitude that creates waiting lists six months or more prior to a peak weekend!

ALLEGHENY FOREST

Details

Check in: 4 p.m. Check out: 11 a.m. Deposit/Cancellation Policy: first night's stay sent within seven days of securing reservation and is non-refundable. If cancellation is made three days prior to date of arrival, a credit is issued for a future visit within one year. If a second cancellation occurs, deposit is forfeited. Payment: cash, personal check, MasterCard, VISA, or American Express. Well-behaved children 8 and older; must be able to sleep in a room by themselves. Rooms accommodate no more than two people. Unsuitable for guest pets. Kennels nearby. Handicap access. Air conditioning in dining room only. Guest rooms have ceiling fans. Private parking for guests.

Rates

$68.90 - $83.74 double occupancy. Weekly rates available. Best to call six months to one year in advance for holidays and peak weekends.

Bed & Bath

Eight intimate guest rooms. Three with private bath in room, five share a separate men's room and ladies' room and shower (no tubs). All rooms have one double bed and are furnished with hand-hewn wormy chestnut beds, calico print quilts or thick comforters, and antique furnishings. A wicker basket filled with complimentary cheese, fruit, crackers and sparkling apple cider is found in rooms. Toiletries and terry robes are provided.

Breakfast & Extras

Served in dining room featuring log walls and beamed ceilings lined with interesting collectibles and 19th-century implements. A wagon-wheel chandelier illuminates the room along with kerosene lamps on each table. Breakfast menu features a choice of pancakes, French toast, catfish and eggs, sausage gravy and biscuits, hot cocoa, spiced tea, and brewed coffee. Dinner served Tuesday through Sunday. The first caller to make dinner reservations for a designated evening chooses the three entrees to be served that day. A la carte menu also available.

Extra Facilities & Features

Space available for corporate retreats and conferences for up to 60 people. Special corporate rate. Facilities for wedding and special occasion receptions. Indoor swimming pool heated to a balmy 92 degrees during winter months with the surrounding concrete floor warmed by an underground heating system. On-site gift shop features country collectibles, Amish-made quilts and gifts. Cross-country skis and ice skates available for rental.

Joseph & Linda Burney

Route 36, Cook Forest, Box 125, Cooksburg, PA 16217. Phone: (814) 744-8017 or (800) 843-6862 (in PA), best to call 7 a.m. - 11 p.m. Location: Jefferson County, off I-80 Exit 13, 16 miles north on Route 36.

KANE MANOR
BED &
BREAKFAST

ew families can claim to have a cast of characters like the Kane family. There's General Thomas Kane, leader of the Union Army Bucktail Division and warrior at the second battle of Bull Run. Before his death, he completed plans for what would become the Kane Manor.

In 1896, his widow Elizabeth and family moved in. Elizabeth, who was northwestern Pennsylvania's first woman doctor, reared four children. Her eldest son, Evan, astonished the medical community by performing surgery on himself twice! Elizabeth's brother-in-law, Elisha, was a noted Arctic explorer, trekking 1300 miles across the Arctic in 1859 searching for a lost crew. During the 1930s, Evan's son, "Sashy," took control of the Manor and converted it into a wayside inn. His risque drawings and cartoons can be found in the Cellar Pub, where guests can get a cup of hot soup and the famous "Passion" drink.

"Sashy" left an amazing array of maps, historical papers, and photographs that cover the attic walls, testimony to world-wide journeys and explorations.

When the Kane family sold its home in 1982, much of the family's memorabilia came with the house, including the thousands of books, generations of family portraits, a seashell collection under glass, heirloom antiques, and two deer trophies gazing down at diners in the Bucktail Room.

Laurie's decorating talents make Kane Manor a cheery establishment. The scenery outside is always breathtaking.

Details

Check in: 2 - 8 p.m. Check out: 11 a.m. Deposit/Cancellation Policy: credit card guarantee to hold room, unless Mystery Clue Weekend, then deposit must be sent. 72 hours notice requested for all cancellations. Payment: cash, personal check, MasterCard, VISA, or American Express. Children welcome. Smoking permitted in designated areas. Unsuitable for guest pets. Kennels nearby. Limited handicap access. No air conditioning, but window fans available. Off-street parking.

Rates

$79 - $110 double occupancy. $110 for suites. $10 for additional person in room. Sleeping bags permitted - extra person charge applies. $25 additional if champagne basket is requested. Best to call one month in advance for peak weekends and holidays. Two-night minimum stay during September, October, January and February weekends.

Bed & Bath

Eleven guest rooms and suites. Seven with private bath, four others share two baths. Rooms have double and/or twin-size beds. Each light and airy room follows a theme matched to its name. Antique furnishings mixed with modern appointments create a comfortable atmosphere. Upon entering, guests will discover welcome bricks, chocolate kisses on the pillows, and if ordered in advance, a champagne basket with cheese, crackers and fruit.

Breakfast & Extras

Served fireside at individual tables in a sun-filled enclosed porch that boasts large windows on three sides, looking out on to the forest's edge. Here diners are often delighted to spot deer coming in to feed on fallen apples and an occasional bear sauntering across the yard. Weekday breakfasts feature a selection of cereals, bagels, homemade muffins, cinnamon bread, fruit and beverages. Saturday and Sunday diners will fill up on entrees that include egg casseroles, blueberry pancakes, peaches-n-cream French toast, home fries, fruit and beverages. Afternoon tea features peanut butter pie and Mudcake. At day's end, guests may enjoy an evening cordial or a glass of wine while mingling with other guests in the Gathering Room.

Extra Facilities & Features

Space available for a corporate retreat of up to 20 participants. Catering for lunch and dinner can be arranged. Special corporate rate. 10 miles of wide trails for hiking and cross-country skiing. Ski equipment available for rental. Trails can be used for biking and hiking in summer months. Swimming and fishing at lake. Boat available for guests. Many theme weekends, including the popular Mystery Clue Weekend. Croquet, badminton and volleyball in summer.

Laurie Anne Dalton,
Innkeeper

230 Clay St., Kane, PA 16735. Phone: (814) 837-6522, best to call afternoons, answering machine other times. Location: McKean County, using I-80 Exit 8 to Route 66 N to 6 E 1 mile or I-80 Exit 18 - 153 W to Route 219 N to Route 321 N to Route 6 E , 2 blocks. Next to Allegheny National Forest, one of Pennsylvania's best-kept secrets.

HEART OF SOMERSET

T his quiet little town atop the Allegheny Mountains is known for its simple, relaxed pace of life. The incredible mountain vistas, scenic farms, and covered bridges have inspired poets, artists and travelers for decades.

The village of Somerset is one of many small mining and agricultural towns in what has become known as the Laurel Highlands.

Many of the charming homes in Somerset date back to the Industrial Revolution, including the Federal-style Heart of Somerset Bed & Breakfast. Built in the 1830s with later Victorian additions, it was owned for over 100 years by the Snyder family, which included prominent local merchants.

The Halversons bought and restored the home in 1988. Now, antiques fill each room, the native pine floors shine and Thomas Edison patent light fixtures grace the lower level.

Guests delight in the interesting stories about the Snyder family. Located within steps of the magnificent County Court House, the home is also part of the walking tour guests can follow at their own pace.

With the variety of area activities available, Ken and Rita encourage guests to mention their areas of interest upon making reservations. One of the most famous historic attractions is Frank Lloyd Wright's Falling Water, only a 30-minute drive. Seven Springs and Hidden Valley ski resorts, water sports, hiking and biking trails are nearby as well.

Details

Check in: 3 p.m. Check out: 11 a.m. (both flexible) Deposit/Cancellation Policy: one-half room rate or guarantee with major credit card. $10 per night cancellation if less than 72 hours notice given. Payment: cash, personal check, MasterCard, VISA, or American Express. No smoking. Unsuitable for guest pets. No handicap access. Central air conditioning. Off-street parking. Somerset Country Inn serves as a "sister" B & B for additional guests.

Rates

$40 - $95 double occupancy. $70 - $110 for suite (seasonally adjusted). $10 charge for additional person in room. Group rates available.

Bed & Bath

Three guest rooms plus a two-room suite. Private and shared baths. Queen or double-size antique beds. Appropriate antique furnishings decorate each room.

Breakfast & Extras

During warmer months guests may choose to enjoy their continental breakfast outside on the porch or in the garden area rather than in the spacious dining room. A typical breakfast includes fresh fruit, pastries, English muffins or toast, a choice of jams and cereals, juice and beverages. Afternoon tea and snacks are available, and evening guests can relax over a glass of wine.

Extra Facilities & Features

Conference space or group of ten to 15. Catering for lunch and dinner can be arranged. Special honeymoon package available.

Ken & Rita Halverson

130 W. Union St., Somerset, PA 15501. Phone: (814) 445-6782, call anytime; leave message if not in; or (800) 638-6693 during weekday office hours (receptionist answers, "Coldwell Banker, Halverson"). Location: Somerset County, in heart of the village of Somerset, 8 blocks from the PA Turnpike Exit 10.

SEWICKLEY BED & BREAKFAST

Thirteen miles from Pittsburgh on the Ohio River, the Asswikales Indian tribe named a charming river town Sewickley or "sweet water." Westward-bound Conestoga wagons and stagecoaches were common 19th-century sights. Riverboat captains and industrial barons alike called it home. The small village atmosphere prevails, church bells ring on Sunday mornings and civic pride endures.

Here, national broadcast and television personality Clark Race and wife, Diane, exchanged their California lifestyle for an 1885 Queen Anne Victorian fulfilling a long-time desire of Clark's — the chance to do a "morning show."

And what a stage! The wrap-around porch, stained-glass windows, handsome woodwork and attention to every detail have created a certain inviting ambiance.

Clark & Diane Race

222 Broad St., Sewickley, PA 15143. Phone: (412) 741-0107, prefer calls from 9 a.m. - 6 p.m., answering machine when not available. Location: Allegheny County, 3 miles north on Route 65 off I-79 Exit 19, minutes from airport and downtown Pittsburgh.

PITTSBURGH

Details
Check in: 4 - 6 p.m. Check out: 1 p.m. Deposit/Cancellation Policy: one night's lodging in advance, returned in full if canceled 48 hours prior to reservation or $20 service fee charged. Payment: personal check, MasterCard, VISA. No children or pets. Kennels nearby. Limited smoking permitted. Cigarette-smoker in residence. No handicap access. Central air conditioning.

Rates
$105 double occupancy.

Bed & Bath
Choice of four guest rooms, with no more than three used at one time. Two guest baths. Three rooms have sinks. Each appointed to a theme and named after favorite musical personalities Clark has worked with during his career. The Mathis Room has a queen-size brass bed, Laine Room has two twin-size canopied beds, Warwick Room has four-poster queen, and Vinton Room has an oversized-king canopy and working fireplace.

Breakfast & Extras
Served fireside in formal dining room, a breakfast that may include Clark's award-winning "Heavenly Hots" (tiny puffy pancakes) or his California scrambles, fruit platter, hot entree with garnishes, baked goods, beverages and juice. Wine and finger foods may be offered in parlor. Complimentary sherry in rooms.

Extra Facilities & Features
There are volumes of books to peruse and a wide assortment of record albums. Films available for viewing on wide-screen TV.

APPLE BUTTER
INN

estled in the rolling green meadows of rural Pennsylvania, this original six-room farmhouse was built in 1844 of bricks formed and fired on the premises. Situated on land granted to encourage westward settlement, it's reputed to have been a stopover for the underground railroad during the Civil War.

The present restoration, begun in 1987 with an architecturally accurate nine-room addition made in 1988, invites guests to experience the charm of a more gracious era. The McKnights' penchant for 19th-century detail is evident throughout the inn. A vented pie-keep serves as a china closet in the drawing room, which also features an 1820 grandfather clock. A wooden apple dryer hangs from the kitchen ceiling.

Guests can enjoy a few quiet moments on the brick deck or wander down to the meadow pond where wild geese frequently land.

Adjacent to the inn is the Wolf Creek School House, an 1899 one-room schoolhouse torn down at its original site and meticulously reconstructed with all of the original woodwork. The addition of a brick fireplace, kitchen and restroom facilities has transformed it into a charming cafe for breakfast and lunch where both inn guests and the general public can enjoy its special ambiance.

The inn is walking distance from Slippery Rock University. Guests can enjoy the rural setting with short trips to local state parks and the Amish country with its many crafts and antique shops.

Details

Check in: 3 - 10 p.m. Check out: 11 a.m. Deposit/Cancellation Policy: a one-night deposit per room is required within seven days of booking. Deposit applies to last day reserved. Deposit will be refunded if cancellation is received one week prior to arrival date. There is a $10 service charge on all cancellations. Payment: cash, personal checks, MasterCard, or VISA. All well-behaved children welcome. No smoking inside. Unsuitable for guest pets, kennel recommendations kindly given. First floor rooms handicap accessible with ramped outside access. One room fully equipped for wheelchairs. Central air conditioning. Off-street parking.

Rates

$75 - $115 double occupancy. $10 - $15 extra person in room. Children's sleeping bags permitted, extra person charge applies. Reservations for holiday weekends best made four weeks in advance.

Bed & Bath

Eleven guest rooms all with in-room private baths (stall showers - no tubs), paddle ceiling fans, televisions, and telephones. Each room decorated with authentic early 1800s antiques, period wall coverings, some with rag rugs and Amish quilts. Beds range in size from double to queen, with one spacious room featuring a king-size bed. Two rooms sleep up to four. Three rooms have working gas-log fireplaces.

Breakfast & Extras

Served in the Wolf Creek School House; guests can choose from a breakfast menu that includes such items as homemade granola, poached apples, banana-oatbran pancakes, and Canadian bacon. Guests may also enjoy afternoon and evening refreshments on the inn's outside deck, sun room, or next to the fireplace in the keeping room.

Extra Facilities & Features

The Wolf Creek School House after 3 p.m. can accommodate groups up to 50. Call inn about rates and catering information. Golfing packages available on private 18-hole country club course.

Kimberly Moses, *Innkeeper*
Sandra & Gary McKnight,
Owners
152 Applewood Lane, Slippery Rock, PA 16057. Phone: (412) 794-1844, best to call 10 a.m. - 10 p.m. Location: Butler County, off Route 173, 7 miles from I-79, Exit 30, 1/4 mile from Slippery Rock University, 50 miles from Pittsburgh, and 75 miles from Erie.

CENTURY INN

When Stephen Hill, a member of the family that founded Scenery Hill, began his years as innkeeper in 1794, George Washington was president of the new republic and the Whiskey Rebellion had citizens from the surrounding countryside in revolt.

Despite this somewhat inauspicious beginning, the inn became a successful venture, welcoming stage coach wayfarers traveling the famed Nemacolin Indian Trail. This same route would later become the great National Road linking the Eastern Seaboard with the western frontier.

As word spread of the notable hospitality offered at the inn, many celebrated persons stopped to experience it firsthand. During General Lafayette's grand tour of the country, his retinue stopped for breakfast in May 1825. A year earlier Andrew Jackson was a guest, returning in February 1826 on the way to his inauguration as president.

The oldest continuously-operated inn along this historic road, attracts guests that are as fascinated by its varied history as they are by its vast array of unusual antiques and excellent cuisine.

A souvenir from the earliest days of operation hangs in the public bar — the only known Whiskey Rebellion flag used by the insurgents at Parkinson's Ferry.

Also on display, in a second-floor room that is open to the public, is an extensive collection of dolls and toys of yesteryear offering visitors a bit of nostalgia at this National Landmark.

Details

Check in: 2 p.m. Check out: 11 a.m. Deposit/Cancellation Policy: $50 deposit sent upon reservation, refunded with seven days' notice. Payment: cash or personal check. No credit cards accepted. Children welcome. Smoking is permitted. Unsuitable for guest pets. Dining room is handicap accessible. Central air conditioning. Off-street parking.

Rates

$75 - $125 double occupancy. Suites $125. $5 for porta-crib or roll-away. Children's sleeping bags permitted, extra charge applies. Best to call three weeks in advance for holidays and peak weekends.

Bed & Bath

Seven guest rooms and two suites, all with private bath. Bridal suite has jacuzzi. Eight rooms have fireplaces, one with private balcony and two with private porch. Bed size varies from twin to king. Furnished with an unusual and rare collection of antiques from many periods. Rooms are equipped with irons and hair dryers. Toiletries provided. Chocolates left in rooms.

Breakfast & Extras

Served in one of five historic dining rooms, to house guests only, a full breakfast that features the chef's choice of the morning. The public bar contains a

display of Monongahela glass while lunch and evening diners enjoy the ambiance of fireside dining with two identical fireplaces flanking a cherry highboy made in 1750.

Extra Facilities & Features

Dinning space for up to 150 in the inn, suitable for corporate luncheons, dinners and wedding receptions. tennis courts, croquet lawn on site.

Megin Harrington

Route 40, Scenery Hill, PA 15360. Phone: (412) 945-5180 or 6600, between noon until 8 p.m. weekdays, until 9 p.m. Friday and Saturday, and until 7 p.m. Sunday, closed mid-December to mid-March. Location: Washington County, I-79 to Route 40 East 9 miles or I-70 to Route 516 South to 40 E, 5 miles. About 50 minutes from Pittsburgh, one hour from Seven Springs.

PRIORY
A CITY INN

The original City of Allegheny, located across the Allegheny River from Pittsburgh, was built on land given to Revolutionary soilders for payment for army service. Later settlers from Germany and Switzerland formed St. Mary's Parish, and in 1852, they built what is now the oldest extant Catholic church in Pittsburgh. In 1888, the priory was added to serve as a home for parish priests and a haven for traveling clergy.

In 1984, after being closed and nearly razed to make way for a new highway, St. Mary's was put up for sale. When the Grafs purchased the complex, they discovered that this was the church Mr. Graf's Swiss grandmother had attended after she emigrated from Winterthur and where his grandparents were married.

The maze of rooms and corridors is distinctly old-world. Mary Ann Graf has added her touches with the decor, antiques and artwork. Guests can relax in the parlor or the library, where the former vault holds an interesting selection of books.

With its convenient location in the historic community of East Allegheny, known as "Deutschtown," visitors can view the Buhl Science Center and Aviary, stroll past the picturesque homes of the Mexican War streets, or explore Pittsburgh's center city minutes away.

The Benedictines believed that a visitor's knock should be responded to with "a prompt answer and the warmth of love." Visitors to the Priory will agree the tradition continues.

Details

Check in: 3 p.m. Check out: 11 a.m., weekdays; 12 noon, weekends. Deposit/Cancellation policy: one night advance deposit unless credit card guarantee is given. Must cancel by 3 p.m. day of arrival or credit card is billed or advance is not returned. Payment: cash, personal check, MasterCard, VISA, American Express, Discover, or Carte Blanche. Children accepted. Smoking is unrestricted. Unsuitable for guest pets. No handicap access. Central air conditioning. Off-street parking.

Rates

$98 double occupancy. $135 for suites. $8 for additional person in room. $10 for roll-aways. Best to call one to two weeks in advance for holiday weekends.

Bed & Bath

Twenty-one rooms and three two-room suites all with private bath and unique in design, authentically appointed with an elegant selection of antiques. Choice of rooms with queen, double, or one twin bed. Combining the charm of the 19th-century with the comforts of the 20th-century, rooms have been provided with toiletries, cable television and phones. Rooms either look out upon old-world courtyard or have an expansive view of the city.

Breakfast & Extras

Served in formal dining room, a continental breakfast that includes two types of cereal, coffee cake, strudel, muffins or bread, fruit, juice and beverages. During warm months rose and Rhine wine is served out on courtyard, while during cold months port and sherry accompanied with light snacks is served in the sitting room from 5 p.m. - 11:59 p.m. Complimentary champagne on New Year's Eve and Valentine's Day.

Extra Facilities & Features

Conference space for up to 25 persons. Fax available. Catering for lunch and dinner can be arranged. Special corporate rate. Garden courtyard ideal for outdoor receptions and informal gatherings. Weekday guests are primarily corporate while weekends are for romantic getaways. Complimentary *USA Today* and weekday morning limousine service to downtown.

Mary Ann Graf

614 Pressley St., Pittsburgh, PA 15202. Phone: (412) 231-3338, can call 24 hours a day for reservations. Location: Allegheny County, just across the Ninth Street Bridge, 1/2 mile from the Golden Triangle and the David L. Lawrence Convention Center.

MAGOFFIN INN

r. James Magoffin of Newry, Ireland, made the difficult decision to move his family to America in 1821. While the rest of the family settled in Kentucky, his eldest son, James, settled down to practice medicine in the town of Mercer. After nearly 50 years of caring for the citizens of Mercer, he was succeeded by his son, Dr. Montrose M. Magoffin. Montrose later married and on September 4, 1885, the local newspaper declared, " . . . the pair will settle in Mercer where the groom has built an elegant new brick residence perhaps the finest in the country, on South Pitt Street, Mercer."

The historic brick home now houses the Magoffin Inn. Located in a quiet town, on a scenic tree-lined street, it sits opposite one of the country's most impressive courthouses.

The Victorian furnishings and appointments envelop guests with a quiet elegance of an era past. Whether visitors come to spend the night or just enjoy a meal, Magoffin's staff works hard to create a warm, friendly environment.

On a side street a block away is the John Orr House, an annex of Magoffin Inn. Built in 1905, it features a handmade brass fireplace insert in the parlor and a carved oak bannister in the front hall.

The Mercer County Historical Society and Museum is next door to Magoffin Inn. Nearby are tennis courts, badminton and a pool free to guests. Hiking and cross-country skiing trails are close by, and the town has many unusual gift and antique shops.

Details

Check in: 2 - 9 p.m. Check out: 11 a.m. Deposit/Cancellation Policy: 50% of room rate required with reservation. Full refund with one week's notice, non-refundable thereafter. Payment: cash, personal check, MasterCard, VISA, or American Express. Children welcome. No smoking inside. Unsuitable for guest pets, kennels nearby. No handicap access. Central air conditioning. Off-street parking.

Rates

$60 - $80 double occupancy. $90 - $110 suites. $10 for additional person in room. Best to call three weeks in advance for holiday and peak weekends.

Bed & Bath

Magoffin Inn has three guest rooms and two suites all with private bath, three with clawfoot tubs and suspended showers. All with well-chosen antique furnishings including many ornate Victorian pieces, several with working fireplaces, private sitting areas and cable television. Toiletries provided. The John Orr House has three guest rooms and one suite. Private and shared baths. Furnishings including colonial antiques and some wicker.

Breakfast & Extras

At Magoffin Inn, meals are served in one of three dining areas, while breakfast is also offered on outside patio during summer months. Breakfast is available to all house guests seven days a week 7 a.m. - 9:30 a.m. and to the public by advance reservation only. The inn serves a full breakfast featuring such items as quiche, French toast, croissants, fruit, juice and hot beverages. Guests staying at the John Orr House enjoy a continental breakfast. Both houses serve the generous Magoffin Muffins. Lunch served from 11 a.m. - 2 p.m. Monday through Saturday. Dnner is available Tuesday through Thursday, family style, from 5 - 8 p.m. and Friday and Saturday, a four-course candlelit affair, from 5 - 8:30 p.m. Reservations advised. Also available at all times to house guests are a selection of cookies, popcorn, party mix, soft drinks, tea or lemonade.

Extra Facilities & Features

Conference space available for up to 25 people. On-site restaurant. Phones in each room. Special corporate rate.

Jacque McClelland, Innkeeper
Gene Slagle, Owner
129 S. Pitt St., Mercer, PA 16137. Phone: (412) 662-4611, 8 a.m. - 8 p.m. Location: Mercer County, five minutes from I-79 Exit 33 or I-80 Exit 2, in heart of Mercer.

MC MULLEN
HOUSE BED
& BREAKFAST

It is doubtful that Celia McMullen, Titusville's first businesswoman, could have ever foreseen the effect oil production would eventually have on the world's economy. It was under her direction that the Petroleum Iron Works Company branched out into the production of heavy oil well drilling tools and became known throughout the world as a manufacturer of high quality equipment.

Befitting her stature in the community, in 1870 she commissioned architect Hiram Smith to design an Italianate villa-style mansion on land purchased from the Watson Petroleum Company. Her home boasted several parlors with marble fireplaces, a large dining room, spacious bedrooms, and servants' quarters.

Over the generations, the mansion has had connections with all phases of Titusville's economic development, from oil production to lumbering to banking. Its present use as a bed and breakfast is significant since tourism is an important service industry in Crawford County.

For visitors attracted to the quaint historic village nestled in the picturesque Oil Creek Valley, McMullen House makes a perfect stopover. It's located just minutes from the Drake Oil Well Museum where visitors can see a replica of the world's first oil rig. It was here in 1859 that Edwin L. Drake drilled the world's first oil well along Oil Creek.

Also nearby is the Oil Creek and Titusville Railroad, offering tours on weekends in May through October. The Allegheny National Forest sports an abundance of outdoor recreation, including fishing, hiking, biking, and cross-country ski trails. A small Amish community is nearby.

Details

Check in: After 4 p.m. Check out: By 11 a.m. Deposit/Cancellation Policy: deposit refunded with 24 hours' notice. Payment: cash or personal check. No credit cards. Children welcome. Cigarette smoking permitted in designated areas, pipes and cigars outside. In residence: two elementary school children, Molly and Casey. Unsuitable for guest pets. Kennel nearby. No handicap access. Central air conditioning throughout inn. Off-street parking.

Rates

$55 - $60 double occupancy. $10 for third person in room. Children's sleeping bag permitted, extra person charge applies.

Bed & Bath

Five spacious guest rooms. Four have private bath in room, one has private bath in hall. All have one double bed, except Maid's Quarters, with two twins. The Yellow Room, with its antique iron bed, also has a working fireplace and private bath in room. Decors vary from Amish to railroad themes. Some antiques. bright, comfortable rooms.

Breakfast & Extras

Served in formal dining room at various tables, the continental breakfast includes a variety of sweet breads and rolls, fresh fruit, juice and beverages. Evening snacks are also offered along with coffee, tea, hot chocolate, and cold beverages.

Charmaine & Eric Rogalski

430 E. Main St., Titusville, PA 16354.
Phone: (814) 827-1592, best between 4 p.m. and 9 p.m., other times answering machine. Location: Crawford County, near Routes 8 and 27 in downtown Titusville, which is south of Erie and east of Meadville.

QUO VADIS

amed after Benjamin Franklin, following the 1859 discovery of oil in nearby Titusville, Franklin soon became a center for worldwide oil production.

Homes built prior to the oil boom were modest in scope, but oil incomes soon produced large, stylish homes such as Quo Vadis. This three-story Queen Anne, is located in Franklin's Historic District and listed in the National Register. The Hoffmans claim they were so impressed with the dining room, parquet floors and woodwork that they ignored the massiveness of the restoration process. Despite all their dilemmas (ask Janean the one about the hallway linen closet), they have created a lovely and comfortable stop for travelers.

In naming their bed and breakfast, Janean chose an expression remembered from Latin class, quo vadis, which means "Where are you going on your travels? Where are you going with your life?" Travelers who find themselves in Franklin will find Quo Vadis a warm, welcoming place to spend the night.

Evenings, guests can wander in to the living room with its electrified log fireplace. Here, the bookcase is filled with a collection of books belonging to an uncle of Janean's who perished in World War I. She has read each of them and encourages guests to browse through and find their own childhood favorite.

For the nostalgia buff, there is a turn-of-the-century Victrola with records to play, plus lots of board games and puzzles and even an upright piano.

Details

Check in: 6 p.m. unless prior arrangements are made. Check out: 11 a.m. Deposit/Cancellation Policy: one night's stay deposit upon reservation, returned if guest calls to cancel before six p.m. day of reservation. Payment: prefer cash or personal check, but accepts MasterCard, VISA, or American Express. Children over 12 welcome. Smoking limited to porch,e. Unsuitable for guest pets, but good kennel within short driving distance. In residence: dachshund Cocoa. No handicap access. No air conditioning but floor and bureau fans are available if needed. Off-street parking.

Rates

$60 - $70 double occupancy. $10 for each additional person in room. Sleeping bags permitted with advance notice. $10 charge applies.

Bed & Bath

Six guest rooms, all with private baths in room. Ground floor room has shower only, five second floor rooms have tub and shower — one with a claw-foot tub and suspended brass shower. Five rooms have one double bed, one room has two double beds. Rooms are furnished with four generations of family heirlooms, Oriental or designer throw rugs, handmade quilts, embroidered bureau scarves with crocheted lace (all made by inn owner's mother and aunt), and at least one antique rocker per room.

Breakfast & Extras

Besides admiring the imposing mahogany sideboard found in the formal dining room, guests can also enjoy the unusual china service, "The Country Diary of an Edwardian Lady," a design adapted from the books and drawings of Edith Holden. Amy's continental breakfast includes fresh squeezed orange juice, fresh fruit, just-baked muffins, sweet breads or coffee cakes and beverages. Afternoons bring the aroma of cookies baking and coffee and tea brewing. Evenings often mark a new batch of fudge or a bowl of freshly popped corn. Upon special request for honeymooners, breakfast can be served in room.

Extra Facilities & Features

Upon departing, guests are given a packet of flower or vegetable seeds to remember their stay at this warm and friendly bed and breakfast.

Bob & Amy Eisenhuth,
Innkeepers
Janean & Allan Hoffman,
Owners

1501 Liberty St., Franklin, PA 16323.
Phone: (814) 432-4208, best to call 9 a.m. -
6 p.m., answering machine on other times.
Location: Venango County, 14 miles north
of I-80, exit 3, north on Route 8 to Franklin.
Inn at corner of 15th and Liberty.

TARA

A uniformed Confederate officer shouting out the morning roll call, the company cook tending an open fire, suspended kettles bubbling over with the noon meal, and men scurrying to line up in military formation for the day's drills. A time warp? Perhaps. But more likely one of the two-day Civil War re-enactments held on the lawns of Tara twice a year.

When the Winners purchased this antebellum house in 1985, it fulfilled their long-time dream of creating a world-class country inn based on the epic movie, "Gone With The Wind."

One hundred and thirty years earlier, in 1854, Charles Koonce chose this quiet country setting along the shores of Lake Shenango to build his three-story Greek Revival mansion. Over the years he had three wives, two of whom, Rachel and Hanna, are buried on the grounds. The Winners accuse Rachel and Hanna of giving them some unexpected help during the 16-month restoration; the wives opened and closed doors and moved items around the house!

Apparently they were pleased with the results because they were not heard from again once guests began arriving at the beautifully-restored antebellum home.

The Winners' attention to detail has accomplished an unparalleled decorating coup, recreating the grace and hospitality of the cherished "Old South," while providing all the expected 20th-century amenities.

In fact, the authentic Southern atmosphere has attracted so much attention that Tara now offers regularly scheduled tours to the public with costumed guides leading the way through the inn's common rooms. The collection of priceless antiques and works of art reflects the lifestyle of a Southern plantation owner.

Details

Check in: 2 p.m. Check out: 12 noon.
Deposit/Cancellation Policy: credit card
guarantee or one night's cash deposit.
Refunded with seven days advance
notice. Payment: cash, personal check,
MasterCard, VISA, or Discover. No
children. Smoking permitted in
designated areas. Unsuitable for guest
pets, kennels nearby. In residence: one
dog of questionable breed, Greta. No
handicap access. Central air
conditioning. Off-street parking.

Rates

$150 double occupancy bed and
breakfast rates. $69 - $99 MAP package
per person, double occupancy.
Additional person for only bed and
breakfast $20. Corporate rates available
Sunday through Thursday. Variety of
package plans. Best to call three months
in advance for peak weekends.

Bed & Bath

Twenty-seven rooms all with private
bath, some with jacuzzis, bidets, sunken
oversized tubs, or clawfoot tubs. All
have fireplaces and sitting areas. The
Garden Suite also has an attached
screened-in porch, reminiscent of an
English garden. Rooms are carefully
furnished to reflect the aura of the
antebellum South with names chosen
for places, characters, or events
portrayed in Gone With The Wind, such
as Mr. and Mrs. Butler's Room with the
neoclassical look of a brass and black
king-size bed, appropriate accessories,
and extra large sunken jacuzzi. Or the
feminine and frilly Fiddle Dee Dee
room, an expression used so often by
Scarlet, with its queen-size canopy bed,
large jacuzzi, and blue and white decor
accented with dozens of frilly bows.
Welcome basket in rooms holds wine,
cheese, and fruit; toiletries in bath, large
terrycloth robes, turn-down service
with chocolate and sherry bedside.

Breakfast & Extras

Served in Ashley's Dining Room, a full
Southern-style breakfast with choices
that include eggs benedict or florentine,
apple cinnamon pancakes accompanied
with a choice of juices, fruit, a pastry
basket and beverages. A continental
breakfast is also available with option of
having it served in the guest room.
Afternoon tea at 4 p.m., wine and cheese
at 6 p.m., and champagne and cider at
check-in. There are three distinct
restaurants on site. Guests may choose
from family-style dining in the Old
South Restaurant, a roadside tavern
"steaks and ale" atmosphere in the
Stonewalls Tavern, or elegant white
glove service in Ashley's Gourmet
Dining Room where a seven-course prix
fixe candlelit dinner is served by staff in
period costume.

Extra Facilities & Features

Conference space available for up to 100
participants. Fax available. Phones in
each room. On-site restaurants for lunch
and dinner. Special corporate rate.
Extensive spa facilities including
swimming, sauna, steam room and
exercise equipment. Outdoor recreation
includes bocci, croquet and boating.
Fifteen golf courses within 15-minute
drive.

Donna & Jim Winner

*3665 Valley View Road, Clark, PA 16113.
Phone: (412) 962-3535, 8 a.m. - 8 p.m.,
answering machine other times. Location:
Mercer County, use I-80 Exit 1 N to Route
18 N, continue 7 miles to PA 258 Exit.*

ABOUT THE AUTHORS

Bruce W. Muncy a native of Dayton, Ohio, studied at Wright State University and received a commercial photography degree from the Ohio Institute of Photography in Dayton. His photography business in Roanoke, Virginia, specializes in architectural photography, product illustration and business portraits. Bruce's work has appeared in "Bed & Breakfast Guide (Southeast)" and in numerous magazines including *National Geographic Traveler, Country Inns, and Innsider*. Bruce has taught at the Winona School of International Photography in Chicago, Illinois, the Georgia School of Photography in Helen, Georgia, and the Ohio Institute of Photography in Dayton, Ohio. Bruce won Virginia's highest photographic award, the *Kodak Award of Excellence,* two consecitive years and was awarded the degrees of *Master of Photography* and *Photographic Crafsman* by the Professional Photographers of America.

Linda C. Feltman, a native of Chicago, Illinois, received her associate degree in business marketing from the College of Dupage and received her B.A. from Penn State's School of Communications. In 1982, Linda and her husband, Brent Peters, began Rest & Repast Bed and Breakfast Reservation Service. In 1987, Linda wrote her first book, "Highways & Byways, Bed and Breakfast in Pennsylvania." She is an active member of the Pennsylvania Travel Council's Bed & Breakfast Division, is on the executive board of the North Central Pennsylvania Bed & Breakfast Association, and serves as the vice president of Centre County's Tourist and Promotion Bureau. She has written numerous articles for state and regional magazines and writes a weekly column on Pennsylvania's bed and breakfasts. Linda has taught several courses and seminars on how to start a bed and breakfast inn.

DIRECTORY TO B & B'S, INNS & RSO'S

Alphabetized by city:

*There are may fine establishments listed here, some known to us but many
we have not visited. We encourage you to write for information and talk
with the innkeepers to be sure their facilities meet your needs and
expectaions.*

PHILADELPHIA COUNTRYSIDE REGION

Brennan's B & B
3827 Linden St
Allentown PA 18104
Lehigh   (215) 395-0869

Coachaus
107-111 N 8th St
Allentown PA 18102
Lehigh (800)-762-8680

Salisbury House
910 E Emmaus Av
Allentown PA 18103
Lehigh   (215) 791-4225

Shamrock House B & B, The
1525 Wynnewood Rd
Ardmore PA 19003
Montgomery   (215) 642-2655

Umble Rest
R. D. #1, Box 79
Atglen PA 19310
Chester   (215) 593-2274

Glen Run Valley View Farm
R. D. #1, Box 69
Atglen PA 19310
Chester   (215) 593-5656

Walnut Hill, B & B at
214 Chandler Mill Rd
Avondale PA 19311
Chester   (215) 444-3703

Hurry Back River House
R. D. #2, Box 2177
Bangor PA 18013
Northampton   (215) 498-3121

Twin Turrets Inn
11 E Philadelphia Av
Boyertown PA 19512
Lehigh   (215) 367-4513

Cottage at the Quiltery
R. D. #4, Box 337
Boyertown PA 19512
Lehigh   (215) 845-3129

Hedgerow B & B
268 Kennett Pk
Chadds Ford PA 19317
Delaware   (215) 388-6080

Hill House
Creek Rd
Chadds Ford PA 19317
Delaware   (215) 388-1596

Casa Del Sol B & B
13 Whitetail Dr
Chadds Ford PA 19317
Chester   (215) 388-7026

Birch Run B & B
R. D. #1, Norway Rd
Chadds Ford PA 19317
Chester   (215) 388-1228

Sevenoaks Farm B & B
492 New Galena Rd
Chalfont PA 18914
Bucks   (215) 822-2164

Old Arcadia Inn
181 Park Av
Chalfont PA 18914
Bucks   (215) 822-1818

Farm View Guest House
R. D. #1, Box 110
Cochranville PA 19330
Chester   (215) 593-6462

Duck Hill Farm
R. D. #1
Downingtown PA 19335
Chester   (215) 942-3029

Pine Tree Farm
Lower State Rd
Doylestown PA 18901
Bucks   (215) 348-0632

Fordhook Farm, The Inn at
105 New Britain Rd
Doylestown PA 18901
Bucks   (215) 345-1766

Highland Farms
70 East Rd
Doylestown PA 18901
Bucks   (215) 340-1354

Pear & Partridge Inn
4424 Old Easton Rd
Doylestown PA 18901
Bucks   (215) 345-7800

Rocky Side Farm
R. D. #1
Elverson PA 19520
Chester   (215) 286-5362

Leibert Gap Manor
4502 S Mountain Dr
Emmaus PA 18049
Lehigh (215) 967-1242

Evermay on the Delaware
River Rd
Erwinna PA 18920
Bucks (215) 294-9100

Isaac Stover House
P. O. Box 68
Erwinna PA 18920
Bucks (215) 294-9861

Duling-Kurtz Inn
146 S Whitford Rd
Exton PA 19341
Chester   (215) 524-1830

Glasbern
R. D. #1, Box 250
Fogelsville PA 18051
Lehigh   (215) 285-4723

Maplewood Farm
P. O. Box 239,
Gardenville PA 18926
Bucks   (215) 766-0477

Crier in the Country
Rt 1, Baltimore Pk
Glen Mills PA 19342
Delaware   (215) 358-2411

Conestoga Horse B & B
R. D. #4, Box 250
Glen Moore PA 19343
Chester   (215) 458-8535

Philadelphia, B & B of
Box 252
Gradyville PA 19039
Philadelphia   (215) 358-4747

Ashmill Farm
P. O. Box 202
Holicong PA 18928
Bucks   (215) 794-5373

Barley Sheaf Farm
Rt 202, Box 10
Holicong PA 18929
Bucks   (215) 794-5104

Arabella
535 Horsham Rd
Horsham PA 19044
Montgomery   (215) 672-0871

Lighted Holly, B & B at
216 N Union St
Kennett Square PA 19348
Chester (215) 444-9246

Clos Normard, Les
773 Marlboro Spring Rd
Kennett Square PA 19348
Chester   (215) 347-2123

Buttonwood Farm
231 Pemberton Rd
Kennett Square PA 19348
Chester   (215) 444-0278

Red Willow Farm
224 E Street Rd
Kennett Square PA 19348
Chester   (215) 444-0518

Meadow Spring Farm
201 E Street Rd
Kennett Square PA 19348
Chester   (215) 444-3903

Punch Run B & B
Unionville-Lenape Rd
Kennett Square PA 19348
Chester   (215) 444-0252

Campbell House
160 E Doe Run Rd
Kennett Square PA 19348
Chester   (215) 347-6756

Bucksville House, The
R. D. 2, Box 146
Kintnersville PA 18930
Bucks   (215) 847-8948

Cornerstone
R. D. #1, Box 155
Landenberg PA 19350
Chester   (215) 274-2143

Meadows, The
501 N Bethlehem Pk
Lower Gwynedd PA 19002
Montgomery   (215) 643-7319

1740 House
River Rd
Lumberville PA 18933
Bucks   (215) 297-5661

Black Bass Hotel
3774 River Rd, Rt 32
Lumberville PA 18933
Bucks   (215) 297-5815

Cuttalossa Cottage
Cuttalossa Farms
Lumberville PA 18933
Bucks

Victorian Retreat B & B
212 W Main St
Macungie PA 18062
Lehigh   (215) 966-4670

Blackberry Hill B & B
295 Boot Rd
Malvern PA 19355
Chester   (215) 647-0554

Eaglesmere Inn
R. R. #3, Box 2350
Malvern PA 19355
Chester   (215) 296-0606

General Warren Inn
Old Lancaster Hwy
Malvern PA 19355
Chester   (215) 296-3637

Fairville Inn
P. O. Box 219
Mendenhall PA 19357
Chester   (215) 388-5900

Elvern Country Lodge
P. O. Box 177
Mount Bethel PA 18343
Northhampton   (215) 588-7922

Minford's Hacienda Inn
36 W Mechanic St
New Hope PA 18938
Bucks

Whitehall Inn
R. D. #2, Box 250
New Hope PA 18928
Bucks   (215) 598-7945

Pineapple Hill
1324 River Rd
New Hope PA 18938
Bucks   (215) 862-9608

Wedgwood Inn, The
111 W Bridge St
New Hope PA 18938
Bucks   (215) 862-2570

Logan Inn
10 W Ferry St
New Hope PA 18938
Bucks   (215) 862-2300

Ramboiullet
Star Rt 83
New Hope PA 18938
Bucks   (215) 862-3136

Back Street Inn
144 Old York Rd
New Hope PA 18938
Bucks   (215) 862-9571

Phillips Mill, The Inn at
N River Rd
New Hope PA 18938
Bucks   (215) 862-2984

Centre Bridge Inn
P. O. Box 74
New Hope PA 18938
Bucks   (215) 862-9139

Hotel Du Village
N River Rd
New Hope PA 18938
Bucks   (215) 862-9911 or 5164

Ye Olde Temperance House
5-11 S State St
Newtown PA 18940
Bucks   (215) 860-0474

Joseph Ambler Inn
1005 Horsham Rd
North Wales PA 19454
Montgomery (215) 362-7500

Little Britain Manor
20 Brown Rd
Nottingham PA 19362
Chester   (717) 529-2862

Log House Inn B & B
15250 Limstone Rd
Oxford PA 19363
Chester   (215) 932-9257

Society Hill Hotel
301 Chestnut St
Philadelphia PA 19106
Philadelphia   (215) 925-1394

Downtown Philadelphia, B & B
728 Manning St
Philadelphia PA 19106
Philadelphia   (215) 923-7349

Thomas Bond House, The
129 S 2nd St
Philadelphia PA 19106
Philadelphia   (215) 923-8523

Chestnut Hill Serenity
8008 Seminole Av
Philadelphia PA 19118
Philadelphia   (215) 248-5219

Welcome Friends B & B
426 E Sedgwick St
Philadelphia PA 19119
Philadelphia   (215) 247-4266

Germantown B & B
5925 Wayne Av
Philadelphia PA 19144
Philadelphia   (215) 848-1375

Genial B & B
2216B Naudain St
Philadelphia PA 19146
Philadelphia   (215) 732-5676

Italian Market Townhouse
817 Mildred St
Philadelphia PA 19147
Philadelphia   (215) 925-9691

Trade Winds
943 Lombard St
Philadelphia PA 19147
Philadelphia   (215) 592-8644

Bell's B & B
33 E Beacon Dr
Phoenixville PA 19460
Chester (215) 933-1561

Valley Forge Garden Spot
137 Forge Hill Ln
Phoenixville PA 19460
Chester   (215) 933-6460

Widow Brown's Inn, The
Rt 611 & Stump Rd
Plumsteadville PA 18949
Bucks   (215) 766-7500

Plumsteadville Inn
Rt 611 & Stump Rd
Plumsteadville PA 18949
Bucks   (215) 766-7500

The Carriage House
Box 172
Point Pleasant PA 18950
Bucks   (215) 297-5367

Stottsville Inn
Strasburg & Valley Rds
Pomeroy PA 19367
Chester   (215) 857-1133

Fairway Farm
Vaughan Rd
Pottstown PA 19464
Montgomery   (215) 326-1315

Coventry Forge Inn
R. D. #2
Pottstown PA 19464
Montgomery   (215) 469-6222

Tattersall Inn
Box 569, Cafferty & River Rds
Pt. Pleasant PA 18950
Bucks   (215) 297-8233

Sign of the Sorrel Horse
R. D. #3, Old Bethlehem Rd
Quakertown PA 18951
Bucks   (215) 536-4651

Kaufman House
Box 183, Route 63
Sumneytown PA 18084
Montgomery   (215) 234-4181

Pheasant Hollow Farm B & B
P. O. Box 356
Thorndale PA 19372
Chester   (215) 384-4694

Whitethorne Farm
842 E Northbrook Rd, Box 92
Unionville PA 19375
Chester   (215) 793-1748

Tara
1 Bridgeton Hill
Upper Black Eddy PA 18972
Bucks   (215) 982-5457

Upper Black Eddy Inn
Rt 32, River Rd
Upper Black Eddy PA 18972
Bucks   (215) 982-5554

Bridgeton House
P. O. Box 167
Upper Black Eddy PA 18972
Bucks   (215) 982-5856

Apple Bucket Country Inn
1245 Old York Rd
Warminster PA 18974
Bucks   (215) 674-1799

Woodhill Farms Inn
150 Glenwood Dr
Washington Crossing PA 18977
Bucks   (215) 493-1974

Quarry House
R. D. #5, Street Rd
West Chester PA 19382
Chester   (215) 793-1725

Highland Manor B & B
855 Hillsdale Rd
West Chester PA 19382
Chester   (215) 696-6251

Crooked Windsor
409 S Church St
West Chester PA 19382
Chester   (215) 692-4896

Old Mill B & B
680 Haines Mill Rd
West Chester PA 19380
Chester (215) 793-1633

Pleasant Roost
1117 N New St
West Chester PA 19380
Chester   (215) 696-2263

Monument House
1311 Birmingham Rd
West Chester PA 19382
Chester   (215) 793-2986

Bankhouse
875 Hillsdale Rd
West Chester PA 19382
Chester   (215) 344-7388

Barn, The
1131 Grove Rd
West Chester PA 19380
Chester   (215) 436-4544

Sleepy Bear B & B, The
140 Myrtle Av
West Grove PA 19390
Chester   (215) 869-3503

Hollilief B & B
677 Durham Rd
Wrightstown PA 18940
Bucks   (215) 598-3100

Wycombe Inn
Box 204, 1073 Mill Creek Rd
Wycombe PA 18980
Bucks   (215) 598-7000

POCONO MOUNTAINS REGION

Beach Lake Hotel
P. O. Box 144
Beach Lake PA 18405
Wayne   (717) 729-8239

East Shore House
P. O. Box 250
Beach Lake PA 18405
Wayne   (717) 729-8523

Bischwind
Box 7, 1 Coach Rd
Bear Creek PA 18602
Luzerne   (717) 472-3820

Toby Valley Lodge
Box 431, Rt 940
Blakeslee PA 18610
Monroe   (717) 646-4893

Indian Mountain Inn
R. D. #1, Box 68
Brackney PA 18812
Susquehanna   (717) 633-2645

Linger Longer B & B
R. D. #1, Box 44
Brackney PA 18812
Susquehanna   (717) 663-2844

Bushkill B & B
P. O. Box F
Bushkill PA 18324
Pike   (717) 588-9118

Overlook Inn
R. D. #1, Box 680
Canadensis PA 18325
Monroe   (717) 595-7519

Nearbrook
Rt 447
Canadensis PA 18325
Monroe   (717) 595-3152

Pump House Inn
Skytop Rd
Canadensis PA 18325
Monroe   (717) 595-7501

Pine Knob Inn
Rt 447, Box 275H
Canadensis PA 18325
Monroe   (717) 595-2532

Dreamy Acres
P. O. Box 7
Canadensis PA 18325
Monroe   (717) 595-7115

Brookview Manor
R. D. #l, Box 365
Canadensis PA 18325
Monroe   (717) 595-2451

Rockgirt B & B
R. D. #2, Box 174A
Canton PA 17724
Bradford   (717) 673-8609

Mmm-Good B & B
R. D. #1, Box 71
Canton PA 17724
Bradford   (717) 673-8153

Fern Hall Inn
R. D. #1, Box 1095
Carbondale PA 18407
Susquehanna   (717) 222-3676

La Anna Guest House
R. D. #2, Box 1051
Cresco PA 18326
Monroe   (717) 676-4225

Ponda-Rowland B & B
R. R. #1, Box 349
Dallas PA 18612
Wyoming   (717) 639-3245

Cherry Mills Lodge
R. D. #1, Box 114A
Dushore PA 18614
Sullivan   (717) 928-8978

Heritage Guest House
R. R. 2078, Box 52
Dushore PA 18614
Sullivan   (717) 928-7354

Eagles Mere Inn
P. O. Box 356
Eagles Mere PA 17731
Sullivan   (717) 525-3273

Rubel B & B
P. O. Box 256
Eagles Mere PA 17731
Sullivan   (717) 525-3027

Shady Lane Lodge
Allegheny Av
Eagles Mere PA 17731
Sullivan   (717) 525-3394

Meadowbrook, The Inn at
Cherry Ln Rd, R. D. #7, Box 7651
East Stroudsburg PA 18301
Monroe   (717) 629-0296

Red Rock Inn
R. D. #7, Box 480
East Stroudsburg PA 18301
Monroe   (717) 421-4976

Georjean's Country Inn
R. D. #1, Box 1214
East Stroudsburg PA 18301
Monroe   (717) 223-9328

Gardners' Inn
R. D. #1, Box 35
Forksville PA 18616
Sullivan   (717) 924-3251

Mc B & B McCarty's B & B
R. D. #1, Box 322
Forksville PA 18616
Sullivan   (717) 924-3374

Mountain Nurseries B & B
Box 106, Thornhurst
Gouldsboro PA 18424
Lackawana   (717) 842-2019

Geese Motif, The
P. O. Box 137
Greeley PA 18425
Pike   (717) 226-0544

Four Counties View B & B
P. O. Box 211
Greentown PA 18426
Pike   (717) 676-3417

Hemlock Grove B & B
R. D. #1, Box 12A
Greentown PA 18426
Pike   (717) 676-4511

Corner House, The
Box 777, Two Pine Stt
Hallstead PA 18822
Susquehanna   (717) 879-4627

Log Cabin B & B
Rt 11, Box 393
Hallstead PA 18822
Susquehanna   (717) 879-4167

Leonard's B & B
Box 393
Hallstead PA 18822
Susquehanna   (717) 879-4167

Lakeside B & B
Lakeside Dr, Pole 285
Harveys Lake PA 18618
Luzerne   (717) 639-2820

Duck Inn, The
Pole 275, Box 547
Harveys Lake PA 18618
Luzerne   (717) 639-2605

Falls Port B & B Inn
538 Academy St
Hawley PA 18428
Wayne   (717) 226-6326

Settlers Inn
4 Main Av
Hawley PA 18428
Wayne   (717) 226-2993

Academy Street B & B
528 Academy St
Hawley PA 18428
Wayne   (717) 226-3430

Tannery House, The
P. O. Box 99, Rt 87
Hillsgrove PA 18619
Sullivan   (717) 928-7354

Olver's B & B
1450 N Main St
Honesdale PA 18431
Wayne   (717) 253-4533

Woodside Mountain House
R. R. #3, Box 1095
Honesdale PA 18431
Wayne   (717) 253-5712

Lausanne House
97 W Broadway
Jim Thorpe PA 18229
Carbon

The Harry Packer Mansion
P. O. Box 228, Packer Hill
Jim Thorpe PA 18229
Carbon   (717) 325-8566

Tiffany's Grand Victoria
218 Center St
Jim Thorpe PA 18229
Carbon   (717) 325-8260

Dimmick House
110 Broadway
Jim Thorpe PA 18229
Carbon   (717) 325-2533

Victoria Ann's B & B
68 Broadway
Jim Thorpe PA 18229
Carbon   (717) 325-8107

Roebling Delaware Inn
Scenic Dr Box 31
Lackawaxen PA 18435
Pike   (717) 685-7900

Liberty Hill
245 E Patterson St
Lansford PA 18232
Carbon   (717) 645-2346

Davies B & B, The
R. D. #1, Box 135A
Mehoopany PA 18629
Wyoming   (717) 833-5307

Sweet Woodruff
201 E Hartford St
Milford PA 18337
Pike   (717) 296-7757

Vines, The
107 E Ann St
Milford PA 18337
Pike   (717) 296-6775

Cliff Park Inn
Milford PA 18337
Pike   (717) 296-6491

Black Walnut Inn
R. D. #2, Box 9285
Milford PA 18337
Pike   (717) 296-6322

Bonny Bank Bungalow
P. O. Box 481
Mill Rift PA 18340
Pike   (717) 491-2250

Montrose House, The
26 S Main St
Montrose PA 18801
Susquehanna   (717) 278-1124

Ridge House
6 Ridge St
Montrose PA 18801
Susquehanna   (717) 278-4933

Woodbourne Farm
R. D. #1, Box 306A-1
Montrose PA 18801
Susquehanna   (717) 278-1395

Farmhouse B & B
HCR 1, Box 6B
Mt. Pocono PA 18344
Monroe

Country Road B & B
HCR1, Box 9-A
Mt. Pocono PA 18344
Monroe   (717) 839-9234

Waltman's B & B
R. D. #1, Box 87
New Albany PA 18833
Bradford   (717) 363-2295

White Cloud Sylvan Retreat
R. D. #1, Box 215
Newfoundland PA 18445
Wayne   (717) 676-3162

Patchwork Farm B & B
R. D. 32, Box 2135
Orwigsburg PA 17961
Schuylkill   (717) 943-2523

Forge B & B, The
R. D. #1, Box 438
Pine Grove PA 17963
Schuykill   (717) 345-8349

Paetzell Haus
211 W. Lockhart St
Sayre PA 18840
Bradford   (717) 888-4748

Park Place B & B
105 Park Pl
Sayre PA 18840
Bradford   (717) 888-5779

Eagle Rock Lodge
Box 265, River Rd
Shawnee PA 18356
Monroe   (717) 421-2139

High Hollow
Star Rt, Box 9-A1
South Sterling PA 18460
Wayne   (717) 676-4275

Sterling Inn
Box 1
South Sterling PA 18460
Wayne   (717) 676-3311

French Manor at S Sterling, The
P. O. Box 39
South Sterling PA 18460
Wayne   (717) 676-3244

Easy Does It Farm
7886 Lincolnway W
St. Thomas PA 17252
Franklin   (717) 369-3891

Nethercott Inn
P. O. Box 26
Starruca PA 18462
Wayne   (717) 727-2211

Maple Hill Farm
R. D., Box 182
Starrucca PA 18462
Wayne

Stroudsmoor Country Inn
P. O. Box 153
Stroudsburg PA 18360
Monroe   (717) 421-6431

Jefferson Inn
R. D. #2, Box 36
Thompson PA 18465
Susquehanna   (717) 727-2625

Burchman House B & B
P. O. Box 420
Thompson PA 18465
Susquehanna   (717) 727-3200

Farm House B & B
Campsite Rd
Thompson PA 18465
Susquehanna   (717) 727-3061

Williamston Inn, The
R. D. #5
Towanda PA 18848
Bradford   (717) 265-8882

Victorian Guest House
118 York Av
Towanda PA 18848
Bradford   (717) 265-6972

Silver Oak Leaf B & B
196 Canton St
Troy PA 16947
Bradford   (717) 297-4315

Sugar Hollow Inn B & B
R. D. #3, Sugar Hollow Rd
Tunkhannock PA 18657
Wyoming   (717) 836-5409

Tyler Hill B & B
P. O. Box 362, Rt 371
Tyler Hill PA 18469
Wayne   (717) 224-6418

Wiffy Bog Farm
R. D. #1, Box 83
Uniondale PA 18470
Susquehanna   (717) 222-9865

Country Mountain Inn B & B
R. D. #1, Box 315
Uniondale PA 18470
Susquehanna   (717) 679-2779

Starlight Lake, The Inn at
Starlight PA 18461
Wayne   (717) 798-2519

Redwood House
Box 9B, E Side Boro
White Haven PA 18661
Luzerne   (717) 443-7186

PA DUTCH HERSHEY AREA REGION

Adamstown Inn
62 W Main St
Adamstown PA 19501
Lancaster   (215) 484-0800

Spring House
Muddy Creek Forks
Airville PA 17302
York   (717) 927-6906

Swatara Creek Inn
R. D. #2, Box 692
Annville PA 17003
Lebanon   (717) 865-3259

Paul Sourss Plantation House
P. O. Box 238
Bendersville PA 17306
Adams   (717) 677-6688

Sunday's Mill Farm
R. D. #2, Box 419
Bernville PA 19506
Berks   (215) 488-7821

Village Inn of Bird-In-Hand
2695 Old Philadelphia Pk
Bird-In-Hand PA 17505
Lancaster   (717) 293-8369

Greystone Manor B & B
P. O. Box 270
Bird-In-Hand PA 17505
Lancaster   (717) 393-4233

Garmanhaus, The
P. O. Box 307
Boiling Springs PA 17007
Cumberland   (717) 258-3980

Jacob's Resting Place
1007 Harnsburg Pk
Carlisle PA 17013
Cumberland   (717) 243-1701

Alwayspring Farm
R. D. #3, Box 480
Carlisle PA 17013
Cumberland   (717) 249-1455

Line Limousin Farm
2070 Ritner Hwy
Carlisle PA 17013
Cumberland   (717) 243-1281

Kellerhaus
1634 Holly Pk
Carlisle PA 17013
Cumberland   (717) 249-7481

Christiansen's Old Barn B & B
1 Main Trail
Carroll Valley PA 17320
Adams   (717) 642-5711

Historic Cashtown Inn, 1797
1414 Old Rt 30
Cashtown PA 17310
Adams   (717) 334-9722

Falling Spring Inn B & B
1838 Falling Spring Rd
Chambersburg PA 17201
Franklin   (717) 776-7179

Winding Glen Farm
R. D. #2, Box 160;
Christiana PA 17509
Lancaster   (215) 593-5535

Foreman House
2129 Main St
Churchtown PA 17555
Lancaster   (215) 445-6713

Old Bridge Inn, The
420 Chestnut St
Columbia PA 17512
Lancaster   (717) 684-3173

Columbian, The
360 Chestnut St
Columbia PA 17512
Lancaster   (1-(800)-422-5869

Hawk Valley, B & B at
R. D. #1, Bxo 59
Denver PA 17517
Lancaster   (215) 445-7658

Yellow House Hotel, The
R. D. #2, Box 170
Douglassville PA 19518
Berks   (215) 689-5433

Danmar House
R. D. #21, Box 107
Dover PA 17315
York   (717) 292-5128

Bechtel Mansion Inn
400 W King St
East Berlin PA 17316
Adams   (717) 259-7760

Red Door Studio, The
6485 Lemon St
East Petersburg PA 17520
Lancaster   (717) 569-2909

West Ridge Guest House
1285 W Ridge Rd
Elizabethtown PA 17022
Dauphin   (717) 367-7783

Wolgemuth's Inn
2832 S Market St
Elizabethtown PA 17022
Lancaster   (717) 367-7907

Elizabethville, The Inn at
30 W Main St
Elizabethville, PA 17023
Dauphin   (717) 362-3476

Elm Country Inn
450 Elm Rd, Box 37
Elm PA 17521
Lancaster   (717) 664-3623

Emig Mansion
Box 486, 3342
Emigsville PA 17318
York   (717) 764-2226

Farmer's Valley
R. D. #4 Box 537
Ephrata PA 17522
Lancaster

Covered Bridge Inn B & B
990 Rettew Mill Rd
Ephrata PA 17522
Lancaster   (717) 733-1592

Clearview Farm B & B
355 Clearview Rd
Ephrata PA 17522
Lancaster

Gerhart House B & B
287 Duke St
Ephrata PA 17522
Lancaster   (717) 733-0263

Hackman's Country Inn
140 Hackman Rd
Ephrata PA 17522
Lancaster   (717) 733-3498

Smithton Inn
900 W Main St
Ephrata PA 17522
Lancaster   (717) 733-6094

Doneckers, Guesthouse at
322-324 N State St
Ephrata PA 17522
Lancaster   (717) 733-8696

Doneckers, 1777 House at
322-324 N State St
Ephrata PA 17522
Lancaster   (717) 733-8696

Kimmell House B & B
851 S State St
Ephrata PA 17522
Lancaster

Fairfield Inn
15 W Main St
Fairfield PA 17320
Adams   (717) 642-5410

Herb Cottage, The
R. D. #2, Box 130
Fayetteville PA 17222
Franklin   (717) 352-7733

Mercersburg Inn
405 S Main St
Mercersburg PA 17236
Franklin   (717) 328-5231

Lantz Farm Home B & B
Box 194, Compass Rd
Gap PA 17527
Lancaster   (717) 442-8229

Fassitt Mansion, The
6051 Old Philadelphia Pk
Gap PA 17527
Lancaster   (215) 383-1928

Ben-Mar Farm Lodging
5721 Old Philadelphia Pk
Gap PA 17527
Lancaster   (717) 768-8353

Goose Chase B & B
200 Blueberry Rd
Gardners PA 17324
Adams   (717) 528-8877

Brafferton Inn, The
44 York Street
Gettysburg PA 17325
Adams   (717) 337-3423

Homestead, The
785 Baltimore St
Gettysburg PA 17325
Adams   (717) 334-2037

Old Appleford Inn
218 Carlisle St
Gettysburg PA 17325
Adams   (717) 337-1711

Twin Elms
228 Bedford Av
Gettysburg PA 17325
Adams   (717) 334-4520

Keystone Inn
231 Hanover St
Gettysburg PA 17325
Adams   (717) 337-3888

Gettystown Inn
89 Steinwehr Av
Gettysburg PA 17325
Adams   (717) 334-9002

Tannery B & B, The
449 Baltimore St
Gettysburg PA 17325
Adams   (717) 334-2454

Doubleday Inn
104 Doubleday Av
Gettysburg Battlefield PA
17325 Adams   (717) 334-9119

Dobbin House Tavern
89 Steinwehr Av
Gettysburg PA 17325
Adams   (717) 334-2100

Tiber House
58 W. Water St
Gettysburg PA 17325
Adams   (717) 332-0493

Herr Tavern and Publick House
900 Chambersburg Rd
Gettysburg PA 17325
Adams   (717) 334-4332

Farnsworth House Inn
401 Baltimore St
Gettysburg PA 17325
Adams   (717) 334-8838

Brierfield B & B
240 Baltimore St
Gettysburg PA 17325
Adams   (717) 334-8725

Bishop's Rocking Horse Inn
40 Hospital Rd
Gettysburg PA 17325
Adams   (717) 334-9530

Castle, The
20 Cottage Av
Glen Rock PA 17327
York

Eagles Nest
P. O. Box 99
Glenville PA 17329
York   (717) 235-2806

Linden Inn
2975 Lincoln Hwy E
Gordonville PA 17529
Lancaster   (717) 687-6532

Osceola Mill House
313 Osceola Mill Rd
Gordonville PA 17529
Lancaster   (717) 768-3758

Mackley Mill B & B
305 S Broad St
Hallam PA 17406
York   (717) 757-6957

Country View Acres
676 Beaver Creek Rd
Hanover PA 17331
York   (717) 637-8992

Beechmont Inn
315 Broadway
Hanover PA 17331
York   (717) 632-3013

Hollybrook
449 N Fairville Av
Harrisburg PA 17112
Dauphin   (717) 657-2348

Gibson's B & B
141 W Caracas Av
Hershey PA 17033
Dauphin   (717) 534-1305

Pinehurst Inn
50 Northeast Dr
Hershey PA 17033
Dauphin   (717) 533-2603

Country Cottage B & B
163 Magnolia Dr
Holtwood PA 17532
Lancaster   (717) 284-2559

Hawk Mountain Inn, The
R. D. #1, Box 186
Kempton PA 19529
Berks   (215) 756-4224

Sycamore Haven Farm
35 S Kinzer Rd
Kinzer PA 17535
Lancaster   (717) 442-4901

Groff Tourist Farm House
R. D. #1, Box 36
Kinzer PA 17535
Lancaster   (717) 442-8223

White Rock Farm Guest House
154 White Rock Rd
Kirkwood PA 19536
Dauphin   (717) 529-6744

Grim's Manor B & B
R. D. #1, Box 341
Kutztown PA 19530
Berks   (215) 683-7089

Walkabout Inn
Box 294, 837 Village Rd
Lampeter PA 17537
Lancaster   (717) 464-0707

Bed & Breakfast - The Manor
830 Village Rd
Lampeter PA 17537
Lancaster

Witmer's Tavern
2014 Old Philadelphia Pk
Lancaster PA 17602
Lancaster   (717) 299-5305

Lincoln House Lodging
1687 Lincoln Hwy E
Lancaster PA 17602
Lancaster   (717) 392-9412

Buona Notte B & B
2020 Marietta Av
Lancaster PA 17603
Lancaster   (717) 295-2597

Meadowview Guest House
2169 New Holland Pk
Lancaster PA 17601
Lancaster   (717) 299-4017

Dingledein House, The
1105 E King Rd
Lancaster PA 17602
Lancaster   (717) 293-1723

Hollinger House B & B
2336 Hollinger Rd
Lancaster PA 17602
Lancaster   (717) 464-3050

King's Cottage, The
1049 E King St
Lancaster PA 17602
Lancaster   (717) 397-1017

New Life Homestead
1400 E King St
Lancaster PA 17602
Lancaster   (215) 396-8928

Wheatland Hills B & B
36 Wilson Dr
Lancaster PA 17603
Lancaster   (717) 393-7452

Nissly's Lancaster City Inns
624-632 W Chestnut St
Lancaster PA 17603
Lancaster   (717) 392-2311

Patchwork Inn
2319 Old Philadelphia Pk
Lancaster PA 17602
Lancaster   (717) 293-9078

Olde Road Apple B & B
2394 Lincoln Hwy E
Lancaster PA 17602
Lancaster   (717) 291-1087

Plant Lovers Tourist Home
1945 Millport Rd
Lancaster PA 17602
Lancaster   (717) 394-2524

Bright Pine Hollow
151 Eshelman Rd
Lancaster PA 17601
Lancaster

Loom Room, The
R. D. #1, Box 1420
Leesport PA 19533
Berks   (215) 926-3217

Sleepy Fir, The
R. D. #2, Box 2802, Ziegler Rd
Leesport PA 19533
Berks   (215) 926-1014

Turtle Hill Road B & B
111 Turtle Hill Rd
Leola PA 17540
Lancaster   (717) 656-6163

Spahr's Century Farm
192 Green Acre Rd
Lititz PA 17543
Lancaster   (717) 627-2185

Swiss Woods
500 Blantz Rd
Lititz PA 17543
Lancaster   (717) 627-3358

General Sutter Inn
14 E Main St
Lititz PA 17543
Lancaster   (717) 626-2115

Alden House, The
62 E Main St
Lititz PA 17543
Lancaster   (717) 627-3363

Banner House B & B
37 E Lincoln Av
Lititz PA 17543
Lancaster   (717) 626-REST

Country Spun Farm B & B
Box 117
Loganville PA 17342
York   (717) 428-1162

Penn's Valley Farm & Inn
Box 385, R. D. #7
Manheim PA 17545
Lancaster (717) 898-7386

Jonde Lane Farm
R. D. #7, Box 657
Manheim PA 17545
Lancaster   (717) 665-4231

Stone Haus Farm
360 S. Esbenshade Rd
Manheim PA 17545
Lancaster   (717) 653-5819

Rose Manor
124 S Linden St
Manheim PA 17545
Lancaster   (717) 664-4932

Herr Farmhouse Inn
2256 Huber Dr
Manheim PA 17545
Lancaster   (717) 653-9852

Country Pines Farm
PA Rt 7, Box 656
Manheim PA 17545
Lancaster   (717) 665-5478

Manheim Manor
140 S Charlotte St
Manheim PA 17545
Lancaster   (717) 664-4168

Landis Farm Guest Home
Gochlan Rd
Manheim PA 17545
Lancaster   (717) 898-7028

Wenger's B & B
571 Hossler Rd
Manheim PA 17545
Lancaster   (717) 665-3862

River Inn, The
258 W Front St
Marietta PA 17547
Lancaster   (717) 426-2290

Vogt Farm
R. D. #1, Box 137A
Marietta PA 17547
Lancaster   (717) 653-4810

Morning Meadows Farm B & B
Furhman Rd
Marietta PA 15747
Lancaster   (717) 426-1425

Olde Fogie Farm
Bainbridge Rd, Box 166
Marietta PA 17547
Lancaster   (717) 426-3992

Three Center Square Inn
Box 428, 3 Center Sq
Maytown PA 17550
Lancaster   (717) 426-3036

New Salem House
Box 24, 275 Old Rt 30
McKnightstown PA 17343
Adams   (717) 337-3520

Guest Farm, The
11335 Punch Bowl Rd
Mercersburg PA 17236
Franklin   (717) 369-2896

Longswamp B & B
R. D. #2, Box 26
Mertztown PA 19539
Berks   (215) 682-6197

Blair Creek Inn
P. O. Box 20, R. D. #2
Mertztown PA 19539
Berks   (215) 682-6700

Gathering Place, The
475 Round Top Rd
Middletown PA 17057
Dauphin   (717) 944-5801

Walnut Hill B & B
801 Walnut Hill Rd
Millersville PA 17551
Lancaster   (717) 872-2283

Greenlawn B & B
150 Letort Rd
Millersville PA 17551
Lancaster   (717) 872-7453

Windy Hill B & B
R. D. #1, Box 240
Mohnton PA 19540
Berks   (215) 775-2755

Mt. Gretna Inn
Kauffman & Pine Sts
Mount Gretna PA 17064
Lebanon   (717) 964-3234

Cameron Estate Inn
R.D. #1 / Box 305
Mount Joy PA 17552
Lancaster   (717) 653-1773

The Country Stay B & B
Box 312 R. D. #1
Mount Joy PA 17552
Lancaster   (717) 367-5167

Green Acres Guest Farm
1382 Pinkerton Rd
Mount Joy PA 17552
Lancaster   (717) 653-4028

Dinner Bell Nook
Schwanger Rd
Mount Joy PA 17552
Lancaster   (717) 653-4909

Cedar Hill Farm B & B
305 Longenecker Rd
Mount Joy PA 17552
Lancaster   (717) 653-4655

Chrisken Inn
4035 Garfield Rd
Mount Joy PA 17552
Lancaster   (717) 653-2717

Donegal Mills
Box 204
Mount Joy PA 17552
Lancaster   (717) 653-2168

Carriage House Manor
143 W Main St
Mountville PA 17554
Dauphin   (717) 285-5497

Nolt Farm Guesthouse
S Jacob St Farm
Mt. Joy PA 17552
Lancaster   (717) 653-4192

Rocky Acre Farm
Rt 3
Mt. Joy PA 17552
Lancaster   (717) 653-4449

Stonebridge Farm
Pinkerton Rd
Mt. Joy PA 17552
Lancaster   (717) 653-4866

Hillside Farm B & B
R. D. #3, Box 627
Mt. Joy PA 17552
Lancaster   (717) 653-6697

Tulpehocken Manor Inn
650 W Lincoln Av
Myerstown PA 17067
Lebanon   (717) 866-4926

Churchtown Inn B & B
2100 Main St
Narvon PA 17555
Lancaster   (215) 445-7794

Farm Fortune
204 Lime Kiln Rd
New Cumberland PA 17070
Cumberland   (717) 774-2683

Memories
R. D. #2
New Freedom PA 17349
York   (717) 235-5554

Lau's B & B
112 Lincolnway E
New Oxford PA 17350
Adams   (717) 624-4972

Hickory Bridge Farm Inn
96 Hickory Bridge Rd
Ortanna PA 17353
Adams   (717) 642-5261

Rose and Crown, The
44 Frogtown Rd
Paradise PA 17562
Lancaster   (717) 768-7684

Rayba Acres Guest Farm
183 Black Horse Rd
Paradise PA 17562
Lancaster   (717) 687-6729

Maple Lane Farm Guest House
505 Paradise Ln
Paradise PA 17562
Lancaster   (717) 687-7479

Verdant View Farm
429 Strasburg Rd
Paradise PA 17562
Lancaster   (717) 687-7353

Neffdale Farm
Strasburg Rd
Paradise PA 17562
Lancaster   (717) 687-7837

Pleasant Grove Farm
R. D. #1, Box 132
Peach Bottom PA 17563
Lancaster   (717) 548-3100

Lake Aldred Lodge
693 Bridge Valley Rd
Pequea PA 17465
Lancaster   (717) 284-4662

Runnymede Farm Guest House
1030 Robert Fulton Hwy
Quarryville PA 17566
Lancaster   (717) 786-3625

Centre Park, The Inn at
730 Centre Av
Reading PA 19601
Berks   (215) 374-8557

Hunter House B & B
118 S 5th St
Reading PA 19602
Berks   (215) 374-6608

Red Lion B & B
101 S Franklin St
Red Lion PA 17356
York   (717) 244-4739

Kurr House
Box 144
Rehrersburg PA 19550
Berks   (717) 933-8219

Springwood B & B
925 Mountain Top Rd
Reinholds PA 17569
Lancaster   (215) 670-1451

Candlelite Inn B & B
2574 Lincoln Hwy E
Ronks PA 17572
Lancaster   (717) 299-6005

Wee Three Guest Home
223 Hartman Bridge Rd
Ronks PA 17572
Lancaster   (717) 687-8146

Calamus Creek Inn
280 Esbenshade Rd
Ronks PA 17572
Lancaster

Benner's Country Home
206 N Ronks Rd
Ronks PA 17572
Lancaster   (717) 299-2615

Franklin House B & B
Main & Market Sts
Shaefferstown PA 17088
Lebanon   (717) 949-3398

Ludwig's B & B
303 W Lancaster Av
Shillington PA 19607
Berks   (215) 777-0004

Field & Pine B & B
2155 Ritner Hwy
Shippensburg PA 17257
Cumberland   (717) 776-7179

Wilmar Manor
303 W King St
Shippensburg PA 17257
Cumberland (717) 532-3784

McLean House
80 W King St
Shippensburg PA 17257
Cumberland   (717) 530-1390

Old Road Guest Home
2501 Old Philadelphia Pk
Smoketown PA 17576
Lancaster (717) 393-8182

Rice's White House Inn
10111 Lincolnway W
St. Thomas PA 17252
Franklin   (717) 369-4224

American House, The
86 Main St
Stouchsburg PA 19567
Berks   (215) 589-5899

Decoy
958 Eisengerger Rd
Strasberg PA 17579
Lancaster   (717) 687-8585

Timberline Lodges
44 Summit Hill Dr
Strasburg PA 17579
Lancaster   (717) 687-7472

Siloan
R. D. #2, Box 82; Village Rd
Strasburg PA 17579
Lancaster   (717) 687-6231

Wye Oak Farm Tourists
R. D. #1, Box 152
Strasburg PA 17579
Lancaster   (717) 687-6547

Limestone Inn
33 E Main St
Strasburg PA 17579
Lancaster   (717) 687-8392

Strasburg Village Inn
1 W Main St, Centre Sq
Strasburg PA 17579
Lancaster   (717) 687-0900

Apple Blossom Inn
117 E Main St
Terre Hill PA 17581
Lancaster   (215) 445-9466

Cook's Guest House
P. O. Box 139
Willow Street PA 17584
Lancaster

Apple Bin Inn B & B
2835 Willow St Pk
Willow Street PA 17584
Lancaster   (717) 464-5881

Green Gables B & B
2532 Willow St Pk
Willow Street PA 17584
Lancaster   (717) 464-5546

Country View Tourist Home
1522 Eshelman Mill Rd
Willow Street PA   17584
Lancaster   (717) 464-4083

Himelhaus B & B
R. D. #1, Box 456
Womelsdorf PA 19567
Berks   (215) 589-4660

Roundtop B & B
R. D. #2, Box 258
Wrightsville PA 17368
York   (717) 252-3169

Johnson's B & B
120 S Beaver St
York PA 17043
York   (717) 845-5096

Smyser Bair House B & B, The
30 S Beaver St
York PA 17401
York   (717) 854-3411

Mundis Mill, The Inn at
586 Mundis Race Rd
York PA 17402
York   (717) 755-2002

Briarwold B & B
R. D. #24, Box 469
York PA 17406
York   (717) 252-4619

Monacacy Manor
R. D. #11, Box 154
York PA 17506
York   (717) 252-2441

VALLEYS OF THE SUSQUEHANNA REGION

Cedar Hill Farm,
Curtinview, Potters Mills
Willows, The
See listing for Rest & Repast

Sunbury Street B & B
Millerstown PA 17062
Perry   (717) 589-7932

Brick House B & B, The
100 E Aaron Sq
Aaronsburg PA 16820
Centre   (814) 349-8795

Plum Bottom Farm
R. D. #1, Box 129
Belleville PA 17004
Mifflin   (717) 935-2981

Hickory Grove B & B
Belleville PA 17004
Mifflin   (717) 935-5289

Grandmaw's Place
R. D. #2, Box 239
Benton PA 17814
Columbia   (717) 925-2630

White House, The
R. D. #2, Box 256-B
Benton PA 17814
Columbia

Irondale Inn
100 Irondale Av
Bloomsburg PA 17815
Columbia (717) 784-1977

Turkey Hill, The Inn at
991 Central Rd
Bloomsburg PA 17815
Columbia   (717) 387-1500

Springfield House B & B
126 E Main St
Boalsburg PA 16827
Centre   (814) 466-6290

Melanie Ann's B & B
120 E Center St
Danville PA 17821
Montour   (717) 275-4147

Colonel Thomas Hartley Inn
Rt 45
Hartleton PA 17829
Union   (717) 922-4477

Cedar Run Inn
Cedar Run PA 17727
Lycoming   (717) 353-6241

Sommerville Farms B & B
R. D. #4, Box 22
Jersey Shore PA 17740
Lycoming   (717) 398-2368

Ye Olde Library B & B
310 S Main St
Jersey Shore PA 17740
Lycoming   (717) 398-1571

Aunt Evie's B & B
R. D. #1, Box 443
Jersey Shore PA 17740
Lycoming   (717) 753-8867

Pineapple Inn, The
439 Market St
Lewisburg PA 17837
Union   (717) 524-6200

Brookpark Farm B & B
R. D. #2, Rt 45
Lewisburg PA 17837
Union   (717) 524-7733

Rogers by the River
308 E Water St
Lock Haven PA 17745
Clinton   (717) 748-1810

Hoffman's Victorian B & B
317 E Water St
Lock Haven, PA 17745
Clinton   (717) 748-8688

Water Co. Farm, The
R. D. #2, Box 108-B
McClure PA 17841
Snyder   (717) 658-3536

Restless Oaks
Box 241
McElhattan PA 17748
Clinton   (717) 769-7385 or
6035

Log Home
R. D. #2, P. O. Box 534
Millville PA 17846
Columbia (717) 458-4681 o

Teneriff Farm B & B
R. D. #1, Box 314
Milton PA 17847
Union   (717) 742-9061

Pau-lyn's Country B & B
R. D. #2, Box 207
Milton PA 17847
Montour   (717) 437-2375

Carriage House at Stonegate,
R. D. #1, Box 11A
Montoursville PA 17754
Lycoming   (717) 433-4340

Bodine House
307 S Main St
Muncy PA 17756
Lycoming   (717) 546-8949

Maple Knoll B & B
Rt 220 N, R. D. #2
Muncy PA 17756
Lycoming   (717) 546-6288

Tressler House, The
41 W Main St
New Bloomfield PA 17068
Perry   (717) 582-2914

Split Pine Farm House B & B
Box 326
Pine Grove Mills PA 16868
Centre   (814) 238-2028

Blue Lion, The
350 S Market St
Selinsgrove PA 17870
Snyder   (717) 374-2929

General Evans Inn, The
R. D. #1, Box 5
Thompsontown PA 17904
Juniata (717) 535-5678

Point House Lodge
Church St
Waterville PA 17776
Lycoming   (717) 753-8707

Thomas Lightfoote Inn
2887 S Reach Rd
Williamsport PA 17701
Lycoming   (717) 326-6396

Reighard House, The
1323 E 3rd St
Williamsport PA 17701
Lycoming   (717) 326-3593

Collomsville Inn B & B
R. D. #3
Williamsport PA 17701
Lycoming   (717) 745-3608

Woodward Inn
P. O. Box 177
Woodward PA 16882
Centre   (814) 349-8118

ALLEGHENY REGION

First Fork Lodge
R. D. #1, Box 74
Austin PA 16720
Potter   (814) 647-8644

Fisher Homestead
253 E Main St
Bradford PA 16701
McKean   (814) 368-3428

Bluebird Hollow
R. D. #4, Box 217
Brookville PA 15825
Jefferson   (814) 856-2858

Kratzer House, Christopher
101 E Cherry St
Clearfield PA 16830
Clearfield   (814) 765-5024

Clarion River Lodge
Box 150, River Rd. / Cook Forest
Cooksburg PA 16217
Forest   (800)-648-6743

Gateway Lodge
Rt 36, Box 125, Cook Forest
Cooksburg PA 16217
Jefferson (814) 744-8017

Au Le Bar's La Shack
R. D. #3, Route 6
Coudersport PA 16915
Potter   (814) 274-7967

Tom and Kathy's B & B
R 144 at Olena
Cross Fork PA 17729
Potter   (814) 435-8582

Inn Town, The
8 W 4th St
Emporium PA 15834
Cameron   (814) 486-1494

Mack Home, The
332 E Allegheny Av
Emporium PA 15834
Cameron   (814) 486-3311

Signor Home, The
336 E Allegheny Av
Emporium PA 15834
Cameron   (814) 486-0795

Jackson Hole East Ranch
R. D. #1, Box 98
Galeton PA 16922
Potter   (814) 435-6710

McDonald's B & B Inn
Box 137
Grampian PA 16838
Clearfield   (814) 236-0306

Wallfarm Country Inn
R. D. Box 503
Grampian PA 16838
Clearfield   (814) 236-1611

Kane Manor B & B
230 Clay St
Kane PA 16735
McKean   (814) 837-6522

Pine-Apple House, The
Star Rt, Box 119
Leeper PA 16233
Clarion   (814) 744-8046

Hill Top Haven
R. D. 1, Box 5C
Liberty PA 16930
McKean   (717) 324-2608

Crossroads B & B
131 S Main St
Mansfield PA 16933
Tioga   (717) 662-7008

Mountain Meadow Farm
P. O. Box 399, Gilfoyle Rd
Marienville PA 16239
Warren   (814) 927-8291

House of Serian
312 W Mahoning St
Punxsutawney PA 15765
Jefferson   (814) 938-3838

Bogert House, The
140 Main St
Ridgway PA 15853
Elk   (814) 773-7185

Dan-D-Don Farm
R. D. #1, Box 400
Sabinsville PA 16943
Tioga   (814) 628-2441

MacBeth's B & B
R. D. #1, Box 42
Sigel PA 15860
Jefferson   (814) 752-2632

Susquehannock Lodge
R. D. #1
Ulysses PA 16948
Potter   (814) 435-2163

Village Inn B & B
Box 152, Main St
Ulysses PA 16948
Potter

Willows B & B
40 Kinzua Rd
Warren PA 16365
Warren   (814) 726-2667

Four Winds
58 West Av
Wellsboro PA 16901
Tioga   (717) 724-6141

Stoplight B & B, The
55 Charleston St
Wellsboro PA 16901
Tioga   (717) 724-4202

Kaltenbach Farm B & B
R. D. #6, Box 106A
Wellsboro PA 16901
Tioga   (717) 724-4954

Auntie M's B & B
3 Sherwood St
Wellsboro PA 16901
Tioga   (717) 724-5771

LAUREL
HIGHLANDS
REGION

Jean Bonnet Tavern
R. D. #2, Box 724
Bedford PA 15522
Bedford   (814) 623-2250

Bedford House
203 W Pitt St
Bedford, PA 15522
Bedford   (814) 623-7171

Vietersburg B & B
1001 E Main St
Berlin PA 15530
Somerset   (814) 267-3696

Buffalo Lodge B & B
R. D. #1, Box 277
Buffalo Mills PA 15534
Bedford   (814) 623-2207

McConnell's Country B & B
Box 174
Clarksburg PA 15725
Indiana   (412) 459-7521

Conifer Ridge Farm B & B
R. D. #2, Box 202A
Clearville PA 15535
Bedford (814) 784-3342

Mountain View B & B
Mountain View Rd
Donegal PA 15628
Westmoreland   (412) 593-6349

Noon-Collins Inn
114 E High St
Ebensburg PA 15931
Cambria   (814) 472-4311

Newry Manor
R. D. #1, Box 475
Everett PA 15537
Bedford   (814) 623-1250

Huntland Farm B & B
R. D. #9, Box 21
Greensburg PA 15601
Westmoreland   (412) 834-8483

Aunt Susie's Country Vacations
R. D. #, Box 225
Hesston PA 16647
Huntingdon   (814) 658-3638

Hoenstine's B & B
418 Montgomery St
Hollidaysburg PA 16648
Blair   (814) 695-0632

Yoders B & B
R. D. #1, Box 312
Huntingdon PA 16652
Huntingdon   (814) 643-3221

Maple Shade B & B
R. D. #1
Huntingdon PA 16652
Huntingdon   (814) 627-0488

Farm Vacation B & B
97 Campbell Ln
Indiana PA 15701
Indiana   (412) 465-7052

Foursquare B & B
Box 221
Indiana PA 15701
Indiana   (412) 465-6412

Meadowbrook School B & B
160 Engbert Rd
Johnstown PA 15902
Cambria   (814) 539-1756

Ligonier Inn
P. O. Box 46, Rt 30 E
Laughlintown PA 15655
Westmoreland   (412) 238-3651

Town House
201 S Fairfield at Loyalhanna
Ligonier PA 15658
Westmoreland   (412) 238-5451

Grant B & B, The
244 W Church St
Ligonier PA 15658
Westmoreland   (412) 238-5135

Mountain Trees B & B
R. D. #1, Box 141
Markleysburg PA 15459
Fayette   (412) 329-1020

Salvinos Guest House B & B
Box 116
Orbisonia PA 17243
Huntingdon   (814) 447-5616

Nationality House
209 Magee Av
Patton PA 16668
Cambria   (814) 674-2225

Fertile Plain, Log Cabin B & B
R. D. #1, Box 98
Pine Bank PA 15354
Greene   (412) 451-8521

Spring Garden Farm
R. D. #1, Box 522
Roaring Springs PA 16673
Blair   (814) 224-2569

Donaldson's Mountain House
Box 204, 14 S Main St
Robertsdale PA 16674
Huntingdon   (814) 635-3833

Trenthouse Inn
R. D. #2
Rockwood PA 15557
Somerset   (814) 352-7713

La Querencia B & B
R. D. #3, Box 127A
Rockwood PA 15557
Somerset   (814) 352-7176

Pine Wood Acres B & B
Rt 1, Box 634
Scottdale PA 15683-9567
Westmoreland   (412) 887-5404

Somerset Country Inn
329 N Center Av
Somerset PA 15501
Somerset   (814) 443-1005

Glades Pike Inn
R. D. #6, Box 250
Somerset PA 15501
Somerset   (814) 443-4978

Heart of Somerset B & B
130 W Union St
Somerset PA 15501
Somerset   (814) 445-6782

Buck Valley Ranch
Rt 2, Box 1170
Warfordsburg PA 17267
Fulton   (717) 294-3759

Robison B & B
Box 247
Wayno PA 15695
Westmoreland   (412) 722-3253

Clover Paradise
R. D. #1
Williamsburg PA 16693
Blair   (814) 832-3201

Waterside Inn
R. D. #1, Box 52
Woodbury PA 16695
Bedford   (814) 766-3776

Woodbury Inn
Box 208, Main Street
Woodbury PA 16695
Bedford   (814) 766-3647

PITTSBURGH
REGION

Garrotts' B & B
R. D. #1, Box 73
Cowansville PA 16218
Armstrong   (412) 545-2432

Hobby Horse Farm
174 Srader Grove Rd
Freeport PA 16229
Armstrong   (412) 295-3123

Gillray Inn, The
Rt 8, Box 493
Harrisville PA 16038
Butler   (412) 735-2274

Shady Elms Farm
R. D. #1, Box 188
Hickory PA 15340
Washington   (412) 356-7755

Flatstone Lick Farm
R. D. #1, Box 121
Marianna PA 15345
Washington   (412) 267-3513

Tavern Lodge, The
101 N Market St, Box 193
New Wilmington PA 16101
Lawrence   (412) 946-2091

Gabriel's B & B
174 Waugh Av
New Wilmington PA 16142
Lawrence   (412) 946-3136

White Oak B & B Guest Home
2400 Willow Dr
North Huntingdon PA 15642
Allegheny   (412) 751-7143

Oakwood
235 Johnston Rd
Pittsburgh PA 15241
Allegheny   (412) 835-9565

Priory - A City Inn
614 Pressley St
Pittsburgh PA 15212
Allegheny   (412) 231-3338

Great Scot Guest House
5923 Kentucky Av
Pittsburgh PA 15232
Allegheny   (412) 661-8348

Century Inn
Rt 40
Scenery Hill PA 15360
Washington   (412) 945-6600

Sewickley B & B
222 Broad St
Sewickley PA 15143
Allegheny   (412) 741-0107

Applebutter Inn
152 Applewood Ln
Slippery Rock PA 16057
Butler   (412) 794-1844

The Candleford Inn B & B
Box 212, Mercer St
Volant PA 16156
Lawrence   (412) 533-4497

Cranberry Corners, Inn at
P. O. Box 503
Warrendale PA 15086
Allegheny

Bird Garden B & B
1415 Mapleview Dr
Washington PA 15301
Washington

Saint's Rest B & B
P. O. Box 15
West Alexander PA 15376
Washington   (412) 484-7950

LAKE ERIE REGION

Bethany Guest House
325 S Main St
Cambridge Springs PA 16403
Crawford   (814) 398-2046

Tara
Rt 18, Box 475
Clark PA 16113
Mercer   (412) 962-3535

Carriage Hill Farm B & B
9023 Miller Rd
Cranesville PA 16410
Erie   (814) 774-2971

The Barnard House B & B
109 River Av
Emlenton PA 16373
Venango   (412) 867-2261

Blueberry Acres
3925 McCreary Rd
Erie PA 16506
Erie   (814) 833-6833

Royal Acre Retreat
5131 Lancaster Rd
Erie PA 16506
Erie   (814) 838-7928

Stonehouse Inn
4753 W Lake Rd
Erie PA 16505
Erie   (814) 838-9296

Quo Vadis
215 Big Oak Dr
Franklin PA 16323
Venango   (814) 432-2877

Villamayer
1027 E Lake Road
Jamestown PA 16134
Mercer   (412) 932-5194

Magoffin Guest House
129 S Pitt St
Mercer PA 16137
Mercer   (412) 662-4611

Stranahan House, The
117 E Market St
Mercer PA 16137
Mercer   (412) 662-4516

Windward Inn
51 Freeport Rd
North East PA 16428
Erie   (814) 725-5336

Ruffles & Roses B & B
290 E State St
Sharon PA 16146
Mercer   (412) 347-4780

McMullen House B & B, The
430 E Main St
Titusville PA 16354
Crawford (814) 827-1592 or 9129

Altheim B & B
104 Walnut St
Waterford PA 16441
Erie   (814) 796-6446

Wilderness Lodge
R. D. #2, Weeks Valley Rd
Wattsburg PA 16442
Erie   (814) 739-2946

RESERVATION SERVICE ORGANIZATIONS

*Each of these RSO's cover
geographic area indicated
with 50-200 inspected properties on
their roster.*

B & B Connections
P. O. Box 21
Devon PA 19333
Chester, Montgomery, Delaware,
Philadelphia, Bucks, and
Lancaster   (215) 687-3565

Chester County, B & B of
Box 825
Kennett Square PA 19348
Chester   (215) 444-1367

Guesthouses, Inc.
R. D. #9
West Chester PA 19380
Southeast PA, Delaware, and NJ
(215) 692-4575

Hershey B & B
P. O. Box 208
Hershey PA 17033
Dauphin   (717) 533-2928

Lancaster County, B & B of
P. O. Box 19
Mountville PA 17554
Adams Berks, Dauphin,
Lancaster   (717) 285-7200

Rest & Repast
P. O. Box 169
Pine Grove Mills PA 16868
Centre, Blair, Huntingdon,
Snyder, & Juniata
(814) 238-1484

Southeast Pennsylvania, B & B of
146 W Philadelphia Av
Boyertown PA 19512
Berks, Bucks, Lancaster
(215) 367-4688

TOURIST PROMOTION AGENCIES

ADAMS COUNTY
Gettysburg Travel Council
35 Carlisle St
Gettysburg PA 17325
(717) 334-6274

ALLEGHENY COUNTY
Greater Pittsburgh Convention
& Visitors Bureau, Inc.
4 Gateway Center
Pittsburgh PA 15222
(412) 281-7711
(800) 255-0855 (in PA)
(800) 821-1888 (outside PA)

ARMSTRONG COUNTY
Armstrong County Tourist
Bureau
402 E Market St
Kittanning PA 16201
(412) 548-3226

BEAVER COUNTY
Beaver County Tourist
Promotion Agency
325 Beaver St
Beaver PA 15009
(412) 728-0212
(800) 342-8192 (Continental U.S.
and Canada)

BEDFORD COUNTY
Bedford County Travel
Promotion Agency, Inc.
P. O. Box 1771
137 E Pitt St
Bedford PA 15522
(814) 623-1771

BERKS COUNTY
Berks County Visitors
Information Association
Vanity Fair Factory Outlet
Complex
Park Road & Hill Av
P. O. Box 6677
Reading PA 19610
(215) 375-4085
(800) 443-6610

BLAIR COUNTY
Convention & Visitors Bureau of
Blair County
1212 Twelfth Av
Altoona PA 16601
(814) 943-8151

BRADFORD COUNTY
Also Sullivan, Susquehanna,
Wyoming
Endless Mountains Association
RR 6, Box 132A
Tunkhannock PA 18657-9232
(717) 836-5431

BUCKS COUNTY
Bucks County Tourist Commis-
sion, Inc.
152 Swamp Rd
Consumer reply - P. O. Box 912,
Department 56
Doylestown PA 18901
(215) 345-4552

BUTLER COUNTY
Butler County Visitors Bureau
100 N Main St, Box 1082
Butler PA 16003-1082
(412) 283-2222

CAMBRIA COUNTY
Cambria County Tourist
Council, Inc.
915 Menoher Blvd
Suite B
Johnstown PA 15905
(814) 536-7993

CAMERON COUNTY
Cameron County Tourist
Promotion Agency
P. O. Box 118
Driftwood PA 15832
(814) 546-2665

CARBON COUNTY
Carbon County Tourist
Promotion Agency
1004 Main St
Stroudsburg PA 18360
(717) 325-3673

CENTRE COUNTY
Centre County Lion Country
Visitors & Convention Bureau
1402 S. Atherton St.
State College PA 16801
(814) 231-1400
(800) 358-5466 (in PA)
Fax : (814) 231-8123

CHESTER COUNTY
Chester County Tourist
Promotion Bureau
117 W Gay St
West Chester PA 19380
(215) 431-6365
(800) 228-9933 (Continental U.S.)
Fax: (215) 344-6999

CLARION COUNTY
Also Jefferson, Clearfield
The Magic Forests of West
Central PA Tourism & Travel
Bureau
c/o Jefferson County Service
Bureau
R. D. #5, Box 101-A
Brookville PA 15825
(814) 849-5197
(800) 348-9393 (Continental U.S.
& Canada)
Fax: (814) 849-5197

CLINTON COUNTY
Clinton County Tourist Promo-
tion Agency, Inc.
Court House
E Water & Jay Sts
Lock Haven PA 17745
(717) 893-4037

COLUMBIA COUNTY
Also Montour
Columbia-Montour Tourist
Promotion Agency, Inc.
121 Paper Mill Rd
Bloomsburg PA 17815
(717) 784-8279

CRAWFORD COUNTY
Crawford County Tourist
Association
P. O. Box 1288
211 Chestnut St
Meadville PA 16335
(814) 333-1258
(800) 332-2338

CUMBERLAND COUNTY
See Dauphin

DAUPHIN COUNTY
Also Cumberland
Harrisburg-Hershey-Carlisle
Tourism & Convention Bureau
114 Walnut St - P. O. Box 969
Harrisburg PA 17108
(717) 232-1377
Fax: (717) 232-4364

DELWARE COUNTY
Delaware County Convention &
Visitors Bureau, Inc.
200 E State St
Suite 100
Media PA 19063
(215) 565-3679
Fax: (215) 565-1606

ELK COUNTY
Elk County Recreation & Tourist
Council, Inc.
159 Main St, Box 357
Ridgway PA 15853
(814) 772-5502

ERIE COUNTY
Tourist & Convention Bureau of
Erie County
1006 State St
Erie PA 16501
(814) 454-7191

FAYETTE COUNTY
See Somerset

FOREST COUNTY
Also Warren
Forest County Tourist Promotion
Agency
P. O. Box 367
Marienville PA 16239
(814) 927-8818
(800) 222-1706 (in PA)

FRANKLIN COUNTY
Cumberland Valley Visitors'
Council
75 S 2nd Street
Chambersburg PA 17201
(717) 261-1200 (for tourist info)
(717) 264-7101

FULTON COUNTY
Fulton County Tourist Promotion
Agency
P. O. Box 141
McConnellsburg PA 17233
(717) 485-4064

GREENE COUNTY
See Somerset

HUNTINGDON COUNTY
Huntingdon County Tourist
Promotion Agency, Inc.
241 Mifflin St
Huntingdon PA 16652
(814) 643-3577

INDIANA COUNTY
Indiana County Visitors &
Convention Bureau
Courthouse Annex
827 Water St
Indiana PA 15701
(412) 463-7505

JEFFERSON COUNTY
See Clarion

JUNIATA COUNTY
Also Mifflin
Juniata-Mifflin County Tourist
Promotion Agency
19 S Wayne St
Lewistown PA 17044
(717) 248-6713

LACKAWANNA COUNTY
Visitors & Convention Bureau
Greater Scranton Chamber of
Commerce
222 Mulberry St
P. O. Box 431
Scranton PA 18501
(717) 342-7711
Fax: (717) 347-6262

LANCASTER COUNTY
Pennsylvania Dutch Convention
& Visitors Bureau
501 Greenfield Rd
Lancaster PA 17601
(717) 299-8901
(800) 735-2629 (Continental U.S.)
Fax: (717) 299-0470

LAWRENCE COUNTY
Lawrence County Tourism
Promotion Agency
Shenango St Station
138 W Washington St
New Castle PA 16101
(412) 654-5593
Fax: (412) 658-0313

LEBANON COUNTY
Lebanon Valley Tourist &
Visitors Bureau
P. O. Box 626
625 Quentin Rd
Lebanon PA 17042
(717) 272-8555

LEHIGH COUNTY
Also Northampton
Lehigh Valley Convention &
Visitors Bureau, Inc.
Terminal Building
P. O. Box 2605
Lehigh Valley PA 18001-2605
(215) 266-0560
(800) 747-0561 (Continental U.S.)
Fax: (215) 266-7127

LUZERNE COUNTY
Luzerne County Tourist
Promotion Agency, Inc.
35 Denison St
Forty Fort PA 18704
(717) 288-6784

LYCOMING COUNTY
Lycoming County Tourist &
Convention Bureau
848 W 4th St
Williamsport Pa 17701
(717) 321-1200
(800) 358-9900 (Continental U.S.)

MCKEAN COUNTY
Seneca Highlands Association,
Inc.
P. O. Box 698
Intersection Rts U.S. #6 and U.S.
#219
Mt. Jewett PA 16740
(814) 778-9944

MERCER COUNTY
Mercer County Tourist Promotion Agency
1 W State St
Sharon, PA 16146
(412) 981-5880
(800) 637-2370 (Continental U.S.)

MIFFLIN COUNTY
See Juniata

MONROE COUNTY
Pocono Mountains Vacation
Bureau, Inc.
1004 Main St
Stroudsburg PA 18360
(717) 424-6050 (tourists)
(800) 762-6667 (Continental U.S.)
Fax: (717) 421-6927

MONTGOMERY COUNTY
Valley Forge Country Conven-
tion & Visitors Bureau
Box 311
Norristown PA 19404
(215) 278-3558
(800) 441-3549 (Continental U.S.)
Fax: (215) 278-5939

MONTOUR COUNTY
See Columbia

NORTHAMPTON COUNTY
See Lehigh

NORTHUMBERLAND
COUNTY
Northumberland County Tourist
Promotion Agency
Human Services Building
370 Market St, Room 308
Sunbury PA 17801
(717) 988-4295
Fax: (717) 988-4444

PERRY COUNTY
Perry County Tourist &
Recreation Bureau
23 Cook Rd
Duncannon PA 17020
(717) 834-4912

PHILADELPHIA COUNTY
Philadelphia Convention
& Visitors Bureau
1515 Market St, Suite 2020
Philadelphia PA 19102
(215) 636-1666 (tourist)
(800) 321-WKND (9563) (tourist,
Continental U.S.)
Fax: (215) 636-3327

PIKE COUNTY
Lake Wallenpaupack
Association
1004 Main St
Stroudsburg PA 18360
(717) 226-2141

POTTER COUNTY
Potter County Recreation, Inc.
P. O. Box 245
Coudersport PA 16915-0245
(814) 435-2290

SCHUYLKILL COUNTY
Schuylkill County Visitors
Bureau
P. O. Box 237
91 S Progress Av
Pottsville PA 17901
(717) 622-7700
(800) 765-7282 (Continental U.S.)
Fax: (717) 622-2903

SNYDER COUNTY
See Union

SOMERSET COUNTY
Also Fayette, Greene, &
Westmoreland
Laurel Highlands, Inc.
Town Hall
120 E Main St
Ligonier PA 15658
(412) 238-5661
(800) 333-5661 (Continental U.S.)
Fax: (412) 238-3673

SULLIVAN COUNTY
See Bradford

SUSQUEHANNA COUNTY
See Bradford

TIOGA COUNTY
Tioga Association for Recreation
& Tourism
Box 56
Mansfield PA 16933
(717) 662-4466
(800) 332-6718 (in PA)

UNION COUNTY
Also Snyder
Susquehanna Valley Visitors
Bureau
Courtyard Offices
Suite 270, Box 2, Rts 11 & 15
Selinsgrove PA 17870
(717) 745-7234
(800) 458-4748

VENANGO COUNTY
Venango County Area Tourist
Promotion Agency
Box 147
315 Main St
Emlenton PA 16373
(412) 867-2472
Fax: (412) 867-5933

WARREN COUNTY
Trivel Northern Alleghenies
315 2nd Avenue
P. O. Box 804
Warren Pa 16365
(814) 726-1222
(800) 624-7802 (15 eastern states)

WASHINGTON COUNTY
Washington County Tourism
59 N Main St
Washington PA 15301
(412) 222-8130

WAYNE COUNTY
Hawley-Lake Wallenpaupack
Chamber of Commerce
1004 Main St
Stroudsburg PA 18360
(717) 226-3191

WESTMORELAND COUNTY
See Somerset

WYOMING COUNTY
See Bradford

YORK COUNTY
York County Convention &
Visitors Bureau
1 Marketway E
P. O. Box 1229
York PA 17405
(717) 848-4000
Fax: (717) 843-6737

"Bed & Breakfast in Pennslyvania" is a quarterly newsletter featuring up-to-date information on Pennsylvania's inns and bed & breakfasts. Yearly subscription is $15.00. Most recent edition is $5.00.

For more information write:
Bed & Breakfast in Pennsylvania
Box 169
Pine Grove Mills, PA 16868